D0255453

MULTINATIONAL
ORGANIZATION DEVELOPMENT

DAVID A. HEENAN
University of Hawaii

HOWARD V. PERLMUTTER
University of Pennsylvania

ADDISON-WESLEY PUBLISHING COMPANY
Reading, Massachusetts • Menlo Park, California
London • Amsterdam • Don Mills, Ontario • Sydney

This book is in the Addison-Wesley series:

ORGANIZATION DEVELOPMENT

Editors:
Edgar H. Schein
Richard Beckhard
Warren G. Bennis

ISBN O-201-02953-7
ABCDEFGHIJ-AL-798

To Our Families

FOREWORD

It has been five years since the Addison-Wesley series on organization development published the books by Roeber, Galbraith, and Steele, and it is almost ten years since the series itself was launched in an effort to define the then-emerging field of organization development. Almost from its inception the series enjoyed a great success and helped to define what was then only a budding field of inquiry. Much has happened in the last ten years. There are now dozens of textbooks and readers on OD; research results are beginning to accumulate on what kinds of OD approaches have what effects; educational programs on planned change and OD are growing; and there are regional, national, and even international associations of practitioners of planned change and OD. All of these trends suggest that this area of practice has taken hold and found an important niche for itself in the applied social sciences and that its intellectual underpinnings are increasingly solidifying.

One of the most important trends we have observed in the last five years is the connecting of the field of planned change and OD to the mainstream of organization theory, organizational psychology, and organizational sociology. Although the field has its roots primarily in these underlying disciplines, it is only in recent years that basic textbooks in "organization behavior" have begun routinely referring to organization development as an applied area that students and managers alike must be aware of.

The editors of this series have attempted to keep an open mind on the question of when the series has fulfilled its function and should be allowed to die. The series should be kept alive only as long as new areas of knowledge and practice central to organization development are emerging. During the last year or so, several such areas have been defined, leading to the decision to continue the series.

On the applied side, it is clear that information is a basic nutrient for any kind of valid change process. Hence, a book on data gathering, surveys, and feedback methods is very timely. Nadler has done an especially important service in this area in focusing on the variety of methods which can be used in gathering information and feeding it back to clients. The book is eclectic in its approach, reflecting the fact that there are many ways to gather information, many kinds to be gathered, and many approaches to the feedback process to reflect the particular goals of the change program.

Team building and the appropriate use of groups continues to be a second key ingredient of most change programs. So far no single book in the field has dealth explicitly enough with this important process. Dyer's approach will help the manager to diagnose when to use and not use groups and, most important, how to carry out team building when that kind of intervention is appropriate.

One of the most important new developments in the area of planned change is the conceptualizing of how to work with large systems to initiate and sustain change over time. The key to this success is "transition management," a stage or process frequently referred to in change theories, but never explored systematically from both a theoretical and practical point of view. Beckhard and Harris present a model which will help the manager to think about this crucial area. In addition, they provide a set of diagnostic and action tools which will enable the change manager in large systems to get a concrete handle on transition management.

The area of organization design has grown in importance as organizations have become more complex. Davis and Lawrence provide a concise and definitive analysis of that particularly elusive organization design—the matrix organization—and elucidate clearly its forms, functions, and modes of operation.

Problems of organization design and organization development are especially important in the rapidly growing form of organization known as the "multinational." Heenan and Perlmutter have worked in a variety of such organizations and review some fascinating cases as well as provide relevant theory for how to think about the design and development of such vastly more complex systems.

As organizations become more complex, managers need help in diagnosing what is going on both internally and externally. Most OD books put a heavy emphasis on diagnosing, but few have provided workable schemes for the manager to think through the multiple diagnostic issues which face him or her. Kotter has presented a simple and workable model that can lead the manager through a systematic diagnostic process while revealing the inherent complexity of organizations and the multiple interdependencies that exist within them.

Human resource planning and career development has become an increasingly important element in the total planning of organization improvement programs. Schein's book provides a broad overview of this field from the points of view of the individual and the total life cycle, the interaction between the career and other aspects of life such as the family, and the manager attempting to design a total human resource planning and development system.

The study of human resources in organizations has revealed the variety of new life-styles and value patterns which employees of today display, forcing organizations to rethink carefully how they structure work and what they consider to be "normal" work patterns. Cohen and Gadon provide an excellent review of various alternate work patterns that have sprung up in the last decade and are revolutionizing the whole concept of a normal work week.

It is exciting to see our field develop, expand, strengthen its roots, and grow outward in many new directions. I believe that the core theory or the integrative framework is not yet at hand, but that the varied activities of the theoreticians, researchers, and practitioners of planned change and OD are increasingly relevant not only to the change manager, but also to line managers at all levels. As the recognition grows that part of *every* manager's job is to plan, initiate, and manage change, so will the relevance of concepts and methods in this area come to be seen as integral to the management process itself. It continues to be the goal of this series to provide such relevant concepts and methods to managers. I hope we have succeeded in some measure in this new series of books.

Cambridge, Massachusetts   Edgar H. Schein
June 1978

PREFACE

Multinationalism has become the password of our times. Whether in the public or private sector, executives around the world stress the importance of their organizations becoming more multinational. But the paths to multinationalism do not come easy—let alone an adequate understanding of the internationalization process of complex institutions. To compound matters, traditional OD approaches are generally unresponsive to the evolving reality of global interdependence.

This book was written to fill this void. Its purpose is to present innovative OD perspectives for the growing number of institutions with international linkages. Its major thesis is that a systematic approach to the processes of *appreciation* (or diagnosis), *planning*, and *intervention* can be applied to the multinationalization of corporations, universities, cities, and nation states. Our approach is social architectural—that is, primary consideration is given to the viability and legitimacy concerns of worldwide institutions.

The scheme of this short volume is as follows:

Part 1 and the first five chapters examine the problems and prospects of building multinational corporations. Our focus is on developing appropriate assessment techniques to evaluate corporate multinationalism, on applying these techniques to major change programs, and on integrating the multinationalization process with the critical objectives of viability and legitimacy.

Chapter 1 introduces a three-stage scenario of the global indus-trial system—a view of the future shared by many leading executives, political spokesmen, and trade unionists. Despite marked transforma-tions in the world economy, we suggest that the multinational cor-poration will remain the key actor for the balance of this century. However, implications of this scenario are also presented for other social institutions.

Chapter 2 considers the meaning of multinationalism. Presented is a taxonomy for all institutions with international linkages: ethno-centric (home-country oriented), polycentric (host-country oriented), regiocentric (regionally oriented), and geocentric (world oriented).

Chapter 3 applies this typology (or EPRG profile) to the decision-making processes of multinational companies. Critical decisions in corporate multinationalization are identified, and specific action plans presented.

The role of the chief executive officer in building a worldwide enterprise is the subject of *Chapter 4*. In the face of rising nationalism and increasing global interdependence, we draw an important distinc-tion between "enclave" geocentrism and "integrative" geocentrism.

Intermediate stages of multinationalism—regiocentrism, in particular—are explored in *Chapter 5*. Regional organizational development and the formation of regional coalitions of private cor-porations are examined.

Part 2 extends our earlier applications of multinational OD to "the global infrastructure"—cities, developing countries, and univer-sities. Case histories are presented of the social architectural approach to multinational appreciation, planning, and intervention.

In *Chapter 6*, we discuss these approaches in four cities: Paris, Coral Gables, Philadelphia, and Honolulu. These experiments high-light how an appropriate multinational role was defined for each city, with particular emphasis on the Honolulu experience.

Chapter 7 describes a unique attempt to encourage private invest-ment in the developmental process of an impoverished country. "Inte-grated Area Development," undertaken in the Philippines' remote Leyte Province, serves as a challenging model for those executives eager to accommodate the viability and legitimacy concerns of emerging nations.

In *Chapter 8*, we consider the difficulties of building worldwide universities. Our primary illustration is the University of Hawaii. But implications are also presented for other higher educators intent on multinationalizing their centers of learning.

Part 3, containing our final chapter, looks briefly ahead to what we might expect in the turbulent world of the future. In our opinion, multinational OD will require a *multiple-nation* as well as a *multi-organizational* approach to the next generation of global problems. To this approach must be added new methods for enhancing the legitimacy of our existing institutions as well as new institutions and networks now missing from the multinational domain.

Our intention is not to offer settled conclusions on the multi-nationalization process. Rather, we hope to identify problems central to building effective worldwide institutions and to indicate how such problems might be lessened.

In so doing, this book summarizes twenty years of collective experience in multinational organization development. For the most part, our collaborative research began in Philadelphia at the Wharton School's Multinational Enterprise Unit. But slowly it has evolved to other parts of the world: from Stockholm to Manila, from Paris to Honolulu. Hopefully, the global reach of multinational OD will be further enhanced by this joint effort.

Honolulu, Hawaii   D.A.H.
Philadelphia, Pennsylvania   H.V.P.
September 1978

ACKNOWLEDGMENTS

We are indebted to many researchers and practitioners for their contributions to this book. Most valuable has been the continued guidance of our Wharton School colleague, Eric L. Trist, who has spent a lifetime improving human conditions in complex organizations. David Sirota was particularly helpful in the methodological segments of Chapters 2 and 3. Several others should be mentioned for their insights on global cities: Hasan Ozbekhan, Ken Smith, Governor Ariyoshi's Committee to Make Hawaii a Regional Center, and the Greater Philadelphia Partnership. Similarly, for their contributions on integrated area development, we would like to thank Sixto Roxas, Victor Ordoñez, Lloyd Vasey, and Marvin Loper.

Our consulting experience and teaching in executive programs have brought us in contact with many executives who have influenced our thinking. While it is difficult to single out any individual, we would like to acknowledge Jose Bejarano, Jacques Maisonrouge, and Calvin Reynolds. In addition, the General Electric, IBM, and Xerox Foundations provided much-needed financial support for various segments of this research.

Transforming our ideas to the printed page was greatly enhanced by the editorial guidance of Richard Beckhard and Edgar Schein. Finally, we are especially grateful to Harriet Yamamoto for her competence, diligence, and unfailing good cheer through successive typings of various drafts of this final product.

The Authors

CONTENTS

Part 1   Building Multinational Companies

1   Introduction

The era of global expansion: 1945–1970 3
The era of unilateral regulation: 1970–early 1980s 5
The era of multilateral regulation: early 1980s–1990s 7
The emerging global industrial system 8
A social-architectural approach to multinational
organization development 12

2   The Meaning of Multinationalism

Definitions abound. 15
The EPRG profile. 21
Strategic implications for MNCs. 22
Summary 26

3   An OD Approach to Multinationalism

Employees as the key actors 27
Suspicions confirmed 31
Root causes of ethnocentrism 36
Reducing ethnocentrism 39
Getting down to critical decisions 42
External stakeholder influences on key personnel decisions 47
Summary 48

4   A Process View of Going Global

Action planning by consensus............................. 50
Special role for CEO.................................... 54
Building separate corporate cultures...................... 59
Beyond the personnel function 61
The inadequacies of introspection........................ 63
The limits of geocentrism 64
Changing concepts of geocentrism 66
Summary 68

5   Regional Organization Development

Significant driving forces 71
Critical factors for success 73
But trust must be earned................................ 77
Regional coalition strategies............................. 79
Further implications.................................... 83
Summary 85

Part 2   Building a Multinational Infrastructure

6   Building Global Cities

A tale of four cities..................................... 93
Tangible and intangible benefits 102
A matter of choice 104
Interesting issues...................................... 106
Analyzing urban competition 114
Building indispensable cities 117
Summary 119

7   Integrated Area Development

Integrated Area Development (IAD)...................... 126
The Honolulu Forum 131
The Manila Forum 138
Summary 140

8   Building Global Universities

The University of Hawaii case........................... 145
Success or failure in multinational OD 157
Concluding note 161

Part 3 The Shape of Things to Come

9   A Look at the Future

The concept of turbulence. 166
Problems at the global level: the RIO approach 167
Bringing the stakeholders inside: managing
organizational problems of the future. 172
Conclusions 178

Appendix: Questionnaires   181

Selected Bibliography   191

PART 1
BUILDING MULTINATIONAL COMPANIES

1
INTRODUCTION

For the next few decades, multinational corporate activity should remain a dominant factor in the global industrial system. But major transformations of the international business phenomenon have been underway for some time and should continue to accelerate through the 1990s. What follows is a cameo of this transformation process.

THE ERA OF GLOBAL EXPANSION: 1945-1970

Since World War II, multinationalism has been on a well-recorded rise. First and foremost were the multinational corporations (or MNCs) intent on reaching world markets.[1] They exported, licensed, sought joint ventures with local firms, or established wholly owned sales and/or manufacturing subsidiaries in as many countries as permitted their presence. Whatever their product, whether razor blades, blue jeans, or first-run movies, their headlong rush abroad transmitted all the material aspects of the home country to foreign soil.

We call this growth period of multinationalism the *era of global expansion* of MNCs. During these years, full-speed ahead internationally was the rule, with contraction or withdrawal from foreign markets synonymous with failure. For the latecomers to international business—most often MNCs from the United States, Japan, and a few emerging nations—the acquisition route was the most realistic and timely way to establish foreign beachheads. It enabled once domestically oriented firms to close the gap between themselves and those companies traditionally committed to overseas markets.

Most important, home and host governments tacitly or overtly supported this expansionary era of multinationalism. Wherever possible, nation-states encouraged the development of MNCs. Relatively speaking, these years could be characterized as a laissez-faire period, and the by-product was a wide diversity of multinational corporations. Consequently, today's business milieu is one of corporate multinationalism, nurtured by twenty-five years of positive attitudes toward the worldwide company.

MNCs come in all sizes and shapes. The smallest tend to be the specialist firms, with products that range from exotic flavors and fragrances to ballpoint pens. On the other end of the spectrum are the megafirms—Exxon, General Motors, IBM, and others—with annual sales in excess of $20 billion.

Most international firms are privately owned. A few, such as Renault of France, are public; while others (British Petroleum and Italian Montedison) have mixed ownership. And ideology seems to make no difference: Russia's Moscow Narodny Bank is an example of many socialist multinationals that have begun to evolve in recent years.

Even the developing countries enter the scene. As a by-product, one now finds twenty-three of the *Fortune non-American 500* represent the Third World—a 200 percent increase over the past five years. One now finds major MNCs based in Brazil, Mexico, South Korea, Hong Kong, and the Philippines, and their capabilities are growing.

Nor has this movement been confined solely to the manufacturing sector. Close on the heels of MNCs was a network of service organizations, consisting of banks, advertising agencies, management consultants, computer software bureaus, and others eager to multinationalize. Later, other organizations, ranging from labor unions to philanthropic agencies, also became convinced that, for them, multinationalization was also a must. Not surprisingly, imaginative and enterprising universities, cities, and even nation-states pursued a parallel course of multinational accommodation.

But the pacesetters of the expansionary era remained the MNCs. For the most part, their focus was inward. As overseas earnings took on added significance, companies became preoccupied with integrating their far-flung operations into some meaningful context, and this boom-or-bust era of multinationalism assumed a rather different shape. As a sign of the times, discussions of global product portfolios became commonplace in corporate boardrooms. Wherever possible, products and services foreign to the domestic market complemented companies' intentions to diversify geographically. Consequently, the challenge of multinational growth became all-consuming as executives around the world stressed the importance of their firms' becoming more multinational.

In a Wharton School survey conducted five years ago, a large percentage of the major United States multinationals indicated that if they had to withdraw from their overseas operations, the impact on their firms would be disastrous.[2] If restrictive legislation on their international activities were passed by the United States Congress, Many American firms even contemplated developing parallel operations overseas with a dual headquarters outside the United States. Similar sentiments were expressed in Western Europe and Japan.

Thus, during this twenty-five year period most executives openly acknowledged a long-term commitment to international business. In evaluating the pros and cons of investing either at home or abroad, senior management in MNCs tended to conclude that the long-term growth opportunities were superior *outside* the parent country.

THE ERA OF UNILATERAL
REGULATION: 1970–EARLY 1980s

By the late 1960s and early 1970s, however, forces of change began to appear—at first, quietly, but persistently nonetheless. The roots of change became visible in at least two domains.

First, local firms intent on multinationalization began to match the competitive edge once held by foreign MNCs. As the latter proliferated, consumers were offered a wider variety of supply at different prices. More often than not, local companies—especially those operating in relatively low-technology industries—began to win back their former customers. A more equal distribution of corporate power began to emerge around the world.

Second, home and host governments, as well as other constituencies, expressed increasing concern over the unregulated activities of multinational companies. Issues concerning irregular and unauthorized payments, inflationary pressures, even the sociocultural impact of foreign investment became increasingly newsworthy. As a corollary, a worldwide resurgence of egalitarianism and concern for human rights caused, and continues to encourage, external groups to reassess the role of MNCs at home and abroad.

One thing has become clear: unfettered expansion and accommodation of MNCs by governments and related constituencies is over. Predictably, the laissez-faire period has given way to the present *era of unilateral regulation.*

While trying to meet the expectations of their citizenry, governments now are increasing their efforts to gain the benefits of corporate multinationalism without its costs. The former image of MNCs as internationalists that reap world markets and distribute the fruits of technology in a rational and efficient manner has given way to a far less flattering one. In many quarters, they are currently viewed as aliens intent on exploiting the locals by virtue of their global reach.

Consequently, multinationals must now cope with a web of regulations on most of their key decisions: pricing, profit remittances, staffing, ownership, technology transfers, and others. Reducing dependence on foreign investment through protective legislation has become the watchword for politicians around the world. And in no small sense, a rise in nationalism fuels these inevitable restrictions on MNCs.

The era of unilateral regulation has led to a new strategic response. MNCs have become much more selective in choosing overseas markets.[3] With increasing precision, they are asking: What are our competitive advantages for the longer term in any given country? What are the relative political risks in particular countries? What governmental responses might be expected for a particular action? These questions are not readily answered. Rather, they prompt considerable introspection in corporate boardrooms.

But the outcomes are predictable. Many overseas operations are closed down or, at least, consolidated. "Rationalization" is the catchword for today's international business person. Renewed interest in the domestic market is apparent and overseas expansion, if any, proceeds on a highly selective basis.

In addition, multinational corporate planners are evidencing renewed interest in environmental scanning and assessing outside forces. External stakeholders—particularly government and labor—are given major attention in charting the future worldwide course of the firm. What emerges from this review is a transformed MNC—an institution prepared to modify policies which may be outdated (such as insistence on wholly owned foreign subsidiaries) in favor of strategies more compatible with the realities of the times. Consequently, *mixed* strategies on key decisions regarding ownership, staffing, and product development are adopted to accommodate varying stakeholder interests.

THE ERA OF MULTILATERAL REGULATION: EARLY 1980s–1990s

Looking ahead, we expect that the era of unilateral regulation will give way to an *era of multilateral regulation* of MNCs. Even today, one sees considerable evidence of such a transformation:

- the multilateral codes of conduct for MNCs recently approved by the Organization for Economic Cooperation and Development (OECD);

- the global guidelines on technological transfers established by the United Nations Commission on Trade and Development (UNCTAD);

- the creation of the United Nation's Centre for Transnational Corporations;

- the rise in commodity cartels, spurred on by the success of the OPEC nations, which will serve as a countervailing force against MNCs;

- the continuing North-South dialogue between the rich and poor nations concerning the role of private investment in the development process.

In each of these cases, the accent will be on heightening *multilateral* surveillance on global companies.

During this period, executives from the private and public sectors should agree on the dominant role of MNCs in facilitating the transition to postindustrialism. In addition, nations should be expected to recognize—emotionally and intellectually—the inevitability of global interdependence. Over time, the distinction between what is a private and what is a public MNC should also become most difficult to draw.

THE EMERGING GLOBAL INDUSTRIAL SYSTEM

What are the implications of this transformation for the MNC? We start with the assumption that both the MNC and the nation-state are institutions capable of an adaptive-learning process, and that effective mechanisms will be developed to cope with the variety of restrictive and permissive public policy and legislative environments likely to occur in the upcoming decades. Multinational corporate activity will not disappear, but the coping process will require fundamental changes in the firm as we know it today.

The nature of these changes is shown in Fig. 1.1.[4] The timetable approximates the periods discussed earlier. As indicated in the figure, the global industrial system includes the totality of interdependent commercial, industrial, and financial activities on the planet Earth. In this perspective the key actor in the multinational domain is the MNC.

Stage I: The Era of National Global Systems

A. *In advanced countries:* Governments encourage buildup of large, national, private and public firms with multinational interests. Regional and global industrial constellations built up.

B. *In lesser-developed countries:* Governments build up control of national economic-industrial system in selected areas with interconnections to advanced-country MNCs (multinational corporate firms).

C. *In socialist countries:* Governments seek a wider transideological zone on a country-by-country basis while working on Comecon multinationals and industrial system constellations.

Stage II: The Era of Bi- and Tri-National and Regional Global Systems

A. *In advanced countries:* Bi- and tri-national companies with global interests (on Dunlop-Pirelli, Unilever, Royal Dutch Shell model). The regional corporations as a dual headquarters for United States and Japanese firms.

B. *In lesser-developed countries:* Bi- and tri-national companies in GISCs (Global Industrial System Constellations) with advanced-country MNCs. A few LAFTA (Latin American Free Trade Association) and ASEAN (Association of South East Asian) multinationals.

C. *In socialist countries:* The transideological firm sanctioned. Comecon plus West European companies merge. Many participate in GISCs.

Stage III: The Era of Geocentric and Geocentroid Global Systems

A. *Key actors:*
   1. Multistate supergiant transideological firms.
   2. Stateless supergiant transideological firms.
   3. Global industrial-financial-commercial-service system constellations and coalitions.

B. *Other actors:*
   1. State-owned MNCs; regional private and mixed MNCs; micro-MNCs; and millions of small non-MNCs. A few large non-MNCs?

C. *Supporting infrastructures:*
   1. Regional and interregional central banks, and a worldwide central bank.
   2. A global financial system—global banking constellations.
   3. Incorporation possibilities in UN or world central bank.
   4. A global patent, tax authority.
   5. World boards for firms with representation of various claimants.
   6. World annual reports with financial, social, ecological impacts of all key actors.
   7. Worldwide shareholding or some new concept of investment.

D. *Other infrastructures:*
   1. Global cities—and regional cities.
   2. Global educational systems and global universities.
   3. Global telecommunication-transportation—persons, ideas, things.
   4. Global arms reduction in relation to global security system.

Fig. 1.1 The emerging global industrial system. (Reprinted by permission from Howard V. Perlmutter, "The Multinational Firm and the Future," *The Annals of the American Academy of Political and Social Science,* September 1972, p. 142.)

Stages I and II are worlds where the nation-state still occupies a prominent role in the identification and ownership of multinational firms. In Stage I, one country exerts a primary influence over each multinational firm, but the firm slips away from home-country control. In Stage II, the main focus of identification is two or more countries or a region. The firm eludes control by any one nation.

Stage III approaches a more truly multinational world, but with powerful controls over multinational corporate activity through the intergovernmental learning process described earlier. Of particular importance in this scenario is the need for new, as yet uncreated, institutions to help in the management of this global interdependence. As we see from Fig. 1.1, global cities and universities are likely outcomes as the nation-state identifies with the changing character of the global industrial system. Other supporting infrastructures in Stage III might include regional, interregional, and global central banks; global patents and tax codes; a global stock exchange; world boards for firms with representation of the various shareholders; and other world-oriented institutions.

A Stakeholder Theory of Viability and Legitimacy

If, during this transformation, the MNC is considered to be a purposeful system—one that transacts with actors who have a stake in its key decisions and outcomes—then the behavior of these key actors or, in our terms, "stakeholders"[5] is critical. In our definition, a *stakeholder* is a group or institution that has one or more of the following features:

- Its contributions—revenues, raw materials, resources, and the like—are vital to the firm.

- It has considerable influence over such important corporate decisions as capital investment, product selection, and return on investment.

- It has the ability to inflict significant damage on the firm if its expectations are not adequately met.

- Its withdrawal of support for the MNC will endanger the survival and performance of the firm.

We distinguish between *external stakeholders,* who are outside the boundary of the firm, and *internal stakeholders,* who are seen as members of the firm.

Management, as one internal stakeholder, has expectations regarding the contributions that it can expect from a major external stakeholder, the host country in which the firm operates. Alternatively, the relevant agencies of the host government have their own expectations of the benefits they are likely to receive from the MNC's activities in their country.

Tensions are inevitable. As invited guests of foreign nation-states, MNCs are obliged to act as good corporate citizens. However, for many firms, this requires special understanding, often not easily obtainable. Take, for example, the case of MNCs from the free-market economies that are introduced to multiple stakeholder roles of the local government. In many host countries where political and economic centralism is king, government's involvement in business may take several forms: as a conegotiator (along with unions in labor relations), as a supplier (where public utilities are state-owned), as a competitor (in the form of quasipublic enterprise), or even as a distributor (where distribution facilities are state-owned). Frequently, executives in MNCs are unable to cope with these special relationships.

As a corollary, there are the special problems of developing countries. Their critical demand for foreign exchange, employment stability, capital investment, and training and development means that a central objective of the firm—short-run profitability—may have to be rationalized. For example, full-scale manufacturing may be insisted on by a host government when, in fact, the local market cannot economically support the necessary level of direct investment. For the firm, the most feasible alternative might be simple assembly operations; but this is unacceptable to the host government. Intense stakeholder conflicts frequently result over such differences of opinion, leading to expropriation of property and even loss of life. Thus, the transactional environment of international business requires matching and accommodating the differing expectations of MNCs and host governments.

Besides attempting to satisfy various foreign governments, an MNC is also responsible to its domestic government. This often presents a double-bind situation for MNCs. On the one hand, for example, a host country might argue that for the firm to remain in the country, it must increase its direct investment. The effect is designed to reduce the country's reliance on imported components, increase local employment, and stimulate exports and foreign exchange. On the other hand, to the home government, this stipulation means the loss of jobs, technology, and investment—all in contradiction to official domestic policy. Thus, the multinational firm frequently walks a tightrope between competing governments.

Governments at home and abroad are not the exclusive stakeholders of multinational firms. Labor unions, competitors, suppliers, consumers, and other interest groups also exert considerable influence on MNCs. What is more, the pressures of a multinational constituency are emerging in strength, and it is important that executives in MNCs perceive their potential significance. Moreover, we look for these key stakeholders to shape the character of the multinational corporations of today and tomorrow.

A SOCIAL ARCHITECTURAL APPROACH
TO MULTINATIONAL ORGANIZATION DEVELOPMENT

Changes in the transactional environment of MNCs can be attributed to changing relationships with both external and internal stakeholders whose contributions to the firm are essential. The critical questions regarding the future of the MNC are *social architectural.*[6]

Social architecture embraces three interdependent activities: theory making, research, and institution building. To paraphrase Lewin's dictum, "There is nothing so practical as a good theory which accounts for the viability and legitimacy of an institution." Important in understanding any social-architectural approach is the distinction between viability and legitimacy.

By *viability,* we mean the degree to which the financial objectives of the firm have been or will be attained. The usual indices of viability include profits, sales, market share, and return on investment or assets managed. Hence, any MNC's viability depends on resource availability and utilization.

Legitimacy refers to stakeholder perceptions that the institution deserves to exist. This occurs, for instance, when the home and host governments believe that MNC is essential in promoting social and economic well-being in their countries. Since legitimacy is confirmed not by management, but rather by external stakeholders, the future of MNCs in many parts of the world will be determined as much for legitimacy reasons as for viability. While formerly a company was considered legitimate if it were viable, today it must demonstrate its legitimacy to groups with the power to affect its viability.

Thus, social architecture is concerned with understanding the conditions under which institutions are perceived by external and internal stakeholders as relatively indispensable. It therefore addresses the fundamental question confronting the MNCs of today and tomorrow: How can worldwide institutions be designed to meet the needs and values of the multiple constituencies in various parts of the world?

Traditional organization development approaches are of limited value in answering this question. With few exceptions, OD represents a planned and systematic approach to improving the internal system of the enterprise through the managed participation of its members. Based on the ongoing learning of organizational participants, OD remains an introspective approach in a world shaped by such externalities as governments, trade unions, customers, and supplies. Where MNCs are concerned, OD applications, at best, have been sketchy. Hornstein and Tichy point out that "OD responses in the past have generally fallen short of dealing with the complexity and magnitude of multinational concerns."[7] And, in our opinion, the limitations of conventional OD in worldwide institution building will increase over time.

By contrast, the social architectural view of multinational organization development is based on the premise that the MNC is a purposeful system, with its viability and legitimacy codetermined by internal and external stakeholders. As a rule, our suggested approach involves identifying the key stakeholders, examining the quality of relationships between stakeholders, and mobilizing their commitment to greater multinationalism. Our objective: to understand existing institutions and to help in some way to design new ones that can keep pace with the fundamental value changes that now influence the global industrial system.

A more complete understanding of the social architectural approach to multinational OD—its similarities and differences with existing theory and practice—should emerge as we proceed in our discussion.

NOTES

1. We shall use the term "MNC." Among other acceptable equivalents are MNE (Multinational Enterprise) and TNC (Transnational Corporation). In a recent United Nations study the Transnational Cor-

poration is acknowledged as the current terminology to all businesses—manufacturing, extractive, agriculture, or service—that operate in another country. Most importantly, this definition now includes TNCs in socialist and developing countries—thus, widening the domain to which our concepts apply. See *The Transnational Corporation in World Development: A Re-examination* (New York: United Nations Economic and Social Council, May 1978).

2. Howard V. Perlmutter, Franklin R. Root, and Leo V. Plante, "Responses of U.S.-Based MNCs to Alternative Public Policy Futures," *Columbia Journal of World Business,* Fall 1973, p. 78.

3. See Sanford Rose, "Why the Multinational Tide is Ebbing," *Fortune,* August 1977, pp. 111–120; Jasbir Chopra, J. J. Boddewyn, and R. L. Torneden, "U.S. Foreign Divestment: A 1972–1975 Updating," *Columbia Journal of World Business,* Spring 1978, pp. 14–18; Stephen Hugh-Jones, "Whatever Happened to the American Challenge?" *The Economist,* September 1977, pp. 139–152; and "Japan's Investment Ardor Cools Off," *Business Week,* October 3, 1977.

4. For a more complete discussion, see Howard V. Perlmutter, "The Multinational Firm and the Future," *The Annals of the American Academy of Political and Social Science,* September 1972, pp. 139–152.

5. Similar stakeholder definitions are developed in Igor Ansoff, *Corporate Strategy* (New York: McGraw-Hill, 1965) and Russell L. Ackoff, *A Concept of Corporate Planning* (New York: Wiley, 1970).

6. See Howard V. Perlmutter, *Towards a Theory and Practice of Social Architecture: The Building of Indispensable Institutions* (London: Tavistock, 1965).

7. Harvey A. Hornstein and Noel M. Tichy, "Developing Organization Development for Multinational Corporations," *Columbia Journal of World Business*, Summer 1976, p. 136.

2
THE MEANING OF MULTINATIONALISM

Multinationalism in complex organizations has yet to be precisely defined. Although the term "multinational" is widely used today, the phrase is still subject to varying interpretations. Practitioners and researchers often use the terms "international," "supranational," "global," "transnational," and "multinational" interchangeably.

DEFINITIONS ABOUND

While some writers have a clear idea of what constitutes a MNC, others have only vague notions. And there is considerable disagreement among internationalists over a satisfactory meaning of multinationalism. Given this lack of consensus, it is not surprising that multiple classification schemes, such as the one described in Fig. 2.1.[1] are currently in vogue.

Objective Criteria

Objective indices, consisting of both structural and performance measures, are usually readily visible and hence quantifiable. The number of overseas offices, foreign languages spoken in the head office, and certain other indices are sacredly held by some observers as the best indicators of a company's true commitment to interna-

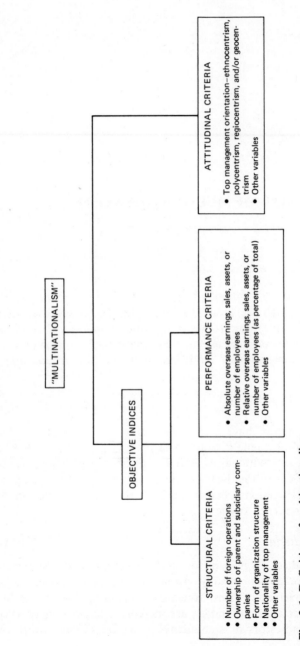

Fig. 2.1 Definition of multinationalism.

tional business. Controversy, of course, rages over the validity of these supposedly objective measures of multinationality. Is a company, for instance, with operations in seven countries really any less multinational than another that operates in ten countries? Probably not. So no matter how useful structural and performance indices are, critics argue that they are not the only definitions of multinationalism, nor are they sufficient ones.

Some of the difficulty in measuring multinationalism with objective indices can be solved by a combination of various measures. One of the authors of this text has argued that: (a) no single criterion of multinationality, such as ownership or the number of nationals overseas, is sufficient and (b) external and quantifiable measures, such as the percentage of investment overseas or the distribution of equity, are useful but not enough.[2]

Attitudes as Fundamental

The more one penetrates the living reality of how decisions are made in a MNC, the more weight must be given to how executives think about doing business around the world. How do they decide who will get important foreign assignments? Analyze various overseas market opportunities? Select a joint-venture partner in a foreign country? Underlying these key decisions are home-country attitudes and beliefs regarding which persons or ideas are competent and trustworthy (foreigners versus compatriots). These attitudes, outlined in Table 2.1, can be labeled ethnocentric, polycentric, regiocentric, and geocentric.[3]

Ethnocentrism refers to a preference for putting home-country people in key positions everywhere in the world and rewarding them more handsomely for work, along with a tendency to feel that this group is more intelligent, more capable, or more reliable. As becomes clear in the banking example presented later in this chapter (see pp. 23–25), ethnocentrism is often not attributable to prejudice as much as to inexperience or lack of knowledge about foreign persons and situations. This is not too surprising, since most executives know far more about employees in their home environments. As one executive put it, "At least I understand why our own managers make mistakes. With our foreigners, I never know. The foreign managers may be better. But if I can't trust a person, should I hire him or her just to prove we're multinational?"

Table 2.1
Four Types of Headquarters Orientation toward Subsidiaries in a Multinational Enterprise

Aspects of the Enterprise	Orientation			
	Ethnocentric	Polycentric	Regiocentric	Geocentric
Complexity of organization	Complex in home country, simple in subsidiaries	Varied and independent	Highly interdependent on a regional basis	Increasingly complex and highly interdependent on a worldwide basis
Authority; decision making	High in headquarters	Relatively low in headquarters	High regional headquarters and/or high collaboration among subsidiaries	Collaboration of headquarters and subsidiaries around the world
Evaluation and control	Home standards applied for persons and performance	Determined locally	Determined regionally	Standards which are universal and local
Rewards and punishments; incentives	High in headquarters; low in subsidiaries	Wide variation; can be high or low rewards for subsidiary performance	Rewards for contribution to regional objectives	Rewards to international and local executives for reaching local and worldwide objectives

Table 2.1 *cont'd.*

Aspects of the Enterprise	Orientation			
	Ethnocentric	*Polycentric*	*Regiocentric*	*Geocentric*
Communication; information flow	High volume of orders, commands, advice to subsidiaries	Little to and from headquarters; little among subsidiaries	Little to and from corporate headquarters, but may be high to and from regional headquarters and among countries	Both ways and among subsidiaries around the world
Geographical identification	Nationality of owner	Nationality of host country	Regional company	Truly worldwide company, but identifying with national interests
Perpetuation (recruiting, staffing, development)	People of home country developed for key positions everywhere in the world	People of local nationality developed for key positions in their own country	Regional people developed for key positions anywhere in the region	Best people everywhere in the world developed for key positions everywhere in the world

The board and top management in the headquarters and affiliated companies are from the home country and have been indoctrinated with the home-country experience. People feel more comfortable with others of similar background, say these managers. Of course, these same attitudes are visible when other vital decisions—like the selection of an overseas banking relationship—are made. Ethnocentric attitudes are universal and no doubt quite resistant to change.

Polycentrism is the attitude that cultures of various countries are quite dissimilar, that foreigners are difficult to understand, and that they should be left alone as long as their work is profitable. In justifying a decision, headquarters executives of such a company might say: "Let the Romans do it their way. We really don't understand what's going on there, but we have to have confidence in them. As long as our foreign managers earn a profit, we want to remain in the background." Local nationals in a polycentric organization occupy virtually all the key positions in their respective local subsidiaries and appoint and develop their own people. Home-country personnel are kept out of these countries. Headquarters, with its holding-company attitude, is manned by home-country nationals who try not to interfere in the territory of each local manager. This low-profile approach of headquarters is justified on managerial and political grounds. Local managers are viewed as having high, if not absolute, sovereignty over their people.

The *regiocentric* attitude sees advantages in recruiting, developing, appraising, and assigning managers on a regional basis. Such a personnel policy is viewed as supportive of functional rationalization on a more-than-one-country basis. For example, a single European production facility may serve several markets. A regional advertising campaign may be launched by Italian, French, British, and German managers with a European orientation. Candidates for positions in European subsidiaries are brought to regional headquarters in Brussels, London, Paris, or Geneva. Despite the continued nationalism of Western European countries, a European team is established with a Eurocentric view. Such an approach has the merit of anticipating emerging politicoeconomic communities, such as the expanded Common Market.

The *geocentric* attitude is evidenced in the attempt to integrate diverse regions through a global systems approach to decision making. Headquarters and subsidiaries see themselves as parts of an organic worldwide entity. Superiority is not equated with nationality. Executives convey in their key decisions the attitude that the distinctive competence of the truly multinational firm is its capacity to optimize resource allocation on a global basis. Good ideas come from any country and go to any country within the firm.

The geocentric approach is not the ideal for all firms with international interests. In practice, it poses a major challenge, given the persistent ethnocentric and polycentric pressures that generally characterize the home and foreign environment of a multinational enterprise. In later chapters, we attempt to clarify the meaning of geocentrism.

THE EPRG PROFILE

The extent to which a worldwide firm exhibits ethnocentrism, polycentrism, regiocentrism, and geocentrism in its key decisions may be thought of as its EPRG profile. No doubt many factors—ranging from the background of the chief executive officer to the firm's history in international business—influence the firm's level of multinationalism. But importantly, all four attitudes usually are demonstrated in varying degrees. It would be both naive and incorrect to state that a firm is ethnocentric or that its product line is geocentric. In the several different companies that have been surveyed, a mix or profile of multinational thinking and behavior can be observed.

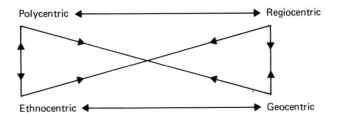

Fig. 2.2 Directions of multinationalism.

Most MNCs probably evolve from ethnocentrism to polycentrism (and later, in some geographical areas, to regiocentrism) and finally to geocentrism. Certainly for those firms intent on international expansion, this appears to be the favored course. But any company—if highly motivated to multinationalize (for instance, with the arrival of a globally minded chief executive officer)—may proceed directly from ethnocentrism to geocentrism. For various reasons (say, the retirement of the same executive), the enterprise may reverse direction from geocentrism back to regiocentrism, polycentrism, or ethnocentrism. Thus, there are several routes to multinationalism.

Stakeholder influences on the EPRG profile, of course, are also considerable. In our present era, this evolution is not so clear. While the geocentric approach may be fostered by organizational changes, such as developing worldwide product divisions that regard the domestic market as just another market, the effect of the external stakeholders on the firm's profile is significant. For example, the ethnocentric approach may be increased by home-government behavior, such as taxation policies on overseas profits or support of defense-related R&D, or by intense pressures from labor unions in times of economic recession and unemployment. The chief executive officer (CEO) may feel the need to pay more attention to the stakeholders of the corporate headquarters than to those from abroad. And since the ownership of most MNCs is mononational, this can also be a basis for legitimizing the ethnocentric approach.

In the era of unilateral regulation, however, pressures from the host-country stakeholders and local-country managers may be in the polycentric direction. Where host-country laws forbid reduction of the working force without permission; where engineering standards are determined locally; and where, on occasion, the government is customer, competitor, and joint-venture partner, the vectors toward polycentrism are considerable. So, whatever the orientation, stakeholder pressures on the firm's multinational profile must be carefully assessed.

STRATEGIC IMPLICATIONS FOR MNCs

To be sure, in exasperation, some executives state, "Who cares how multinational we are as long as we're profitable?" Even though limited empirical evidence indicates that a positive correlation between multinationalization and profitability exists, perceptions count. Executives around the world closely associate paying greater attention to international operations with improvement of corporate performance. These individuals point to the experiences of their own companies as incentives to multinationalize. Consider, for example, the following case history of one of our clients.

Case A

A few years ago, a large bank faced serious difficulties in competing with other international banks. Even though it had a seventy-year history in foreign operations and its overseas business contributed over 35 percent of total earnings, other American banks were consistently eroding the bank's international market share. Nowhere was this more evident than in its primary customer segment, United States multinationals conducting business abroad.

While senior executives often defended their company as one with "a truly multinational perspective," its major critics—both within and outside the organization—categorized the firm as "essentially an American bank that *happens* to be involved in international business." Others remarked, "It's a great domestic bank. But internationally, it's out of touch and badly lags behind the competition!" A predominantly ethnocentric attitude, to the exclusion of outside ideas and concepts, pervaded the bank's thinking and was manifested in many ways. As an example, its overseas staffing policies placed a heavy (almost exclusive) reliance on United States expatriates because, in the bank's terms, "our American clients simply insist on doing business with other Americans." However, interviews with the comptrollers of United States MNCs clearly revealed this perceived need did not exist. Potential bank clients expressed their major concern as one of "availability of adequate financing . . . at suitable terms," with little or no premium placed on the American citizenship of bank lending officers. This is simply one of many indications of the bank's failure to gauge accurately its major international market segment.

Constraints in the legal and economic environment of international banking further aggravated the bank's home-country orientation. A major restriction on all United States banks operating overseas is the limited number of retail branches they are allowed to establish. Whereas at home a bank may have the advantages of an extensive branch network (including perhaps over 1,000 units), it is usually limited to a very few branches in the host country. This makes it very difficult for the overseas affiliates of U.S. banks to generate sufficient funds to satisfy the extensive loan demands of those MNCs intent on expanding their foreign operations. Alternative sourcing methods, therefore, become critical.

Take, for instance, our client bank's problems in Japan. Limited to two retail branches—one in Tokyo, the other in Osaka—the bank sought out other sources to fuel the intensive lending appetites of potential American multinational customers. As a result, a strategy was proposed of attracting the deposits of high-cash-flow United States MNCs in Japan. In particular, the food and insurance industries were singled out. As indicated below, they were potentially heavy net suppliers of funds—funds that eventually could be translated into profitable industrial loans to heavy users in the textile, petroleum, and transportation industries.

Industry	Deposit: Loan Ratio
Food	**1:0.1**
Insurance	**1:0.2**
Machinery	1:3.2
Services	1:3.7
Primary metals	1:5.0
Fabricated metals	1:5.5
Electrical	1:6.0
Chemicals	1:6.7
Textiles	1:7.5
Petroleum	1:8.4
Transportation	1:15.0

Unfortunately, in this bank's case, very limited relations had been developed with either the food or the insurance industry. The bank had established the primary or "lead relationship" with only two of eighteen major American food companies operating in Japan. The same for insurance, where less than $100,000 in deposits had been gathered, even though Amrican life-insurance firms in Japan had underwritten $83 million in contracts during the previous year!

Even more disappointing was the bank's inability to retain in Japan the accounts of United States MNCs that had a long-standing lead relationship with the bank in New York. And furthermore, this finding occurred in virtually every overseas market where the bank conducted its business. There was a total lack of continuity of account relationships across national boundaries. Almost without exception, the bank's executives in the head office and overseas failed to sense the rising multinationality of its customer base. Information regarding client needs or trends around the world was never exchanged by key officers in the bank. Accordingly, its level of service suffered, with the loss of many important accounts as a major consequence.

As early as 1970, we recommended to the company a geocentric framework for overseeing its international business. This was to take the form of a Multinational Corporation Division in the bank to coordinate the financial needs of worldwide companies. If a particular customer's Indonesian refining operations were to be expanded, this information would be received into such a system and appropriate bank action taken. Similarly, if a divestment were being considered by its Peruvian subsidiary, the proper banking responses would also be made. Through such a division, global clients of the bank would be treated as parts of an organic worldwide entity and an integrated and comprehensive set of financial options would be provided on an ongoing basis.

Unfortunately, our recommendations were not heeded, and the bank continued to treat its foreign operations as an appendage of its domestic business. More importantly, several of its major competitors developed World Corporation Groups shortly thereafter along the lines we had suggested earlier to our client, with rather spectacular results.

With such examples in mind, most executives attest to their desire to make their firms truly multinational. They argue that a cadre of managers with truly global attitudes would, in theory at least, make it possible for a MNC to find better answers to such important questions as: Where in the world shall we build that plant? How are we going to raise the money? Where can we find suppliers of the materials and resources we need? Where can we get the technology to give us the edge we want? Managers in MNCs recognize that finding the correct answers to these questions is crucial to maintaining a good position in the global marketplace. Furthermore, executives sense that before a company can achieve a truly multinational level, it is necessary to know exactly what that entails.

SUMMARY

This chapter focused on the dynamic effects of multinationalism and its strategic implications. An attitudinal definition of multinationality was presented. This taxonomy considers the degree to which decision making in MNCs is ethnocentric (home-country oriented), polycentric (host-country oriented), regiocentric (regionally oriented), or geocentric (globally oriented). A firm's EPRG profile reveals the nature of its commitment to multinationalism. Subsequent chapters discuss the operational aspects of these concepts, with case studies presented.

NOTES

1. Yair Aharoni, "On the Definition of a Multinational Corporation," *Quarterly Review of Economics and Business* 2 (1971): 14.

2. Howard V. Perlmutter, "The Tortuous Evolution of the Multinational Corporation," *Columbia Journal of World Business,* January–February 1969, p. 12.

3. Howard V. Perlmutter and David A. Heenan, "How Multinational Should Your Top Managers Be?" *Harvard Business Review,* November–December 1974, p. 121.

3
AN OD APPROACH TO MULTINATIONALISM

To monitor institutional progress toward multinationalism, the Multi-national Measurement Program was established at the Wharton School of the University of Pennsylvania. Begun in 1970, this program was part of a more comprehensive MOD effort designed to enhance the survival, growth, and profitability of firms by accelerating their rate of multinationalization. For the most part, this meant shifting the EPRG profile of organizations through scheduled interventions. And, with few exceptions, entry was at the CEO level in MNCs experiencing some of the difficulties mentioned in Chapter 2.

EMPLOYEES AS THE KEY ACTORS

For the next several years at least, insiders—employees and shareholders—should probably be considered the key actors in any major change process. Building viable worldwide institutions through the 1970s requires the personalized commitment of participating managers on such sensitive issues as planning their own careers, structuring new organizational relationships, and defining the basic character of their companies.

To lead off our change program, we asked these executives where the drive for multinationalism ought best to begin in their companies. Invariably, senior management identified the human factor as the best point of departure. As one chief executive officer said, "If we can't multinationalize our management, then it doesn't make much sense to feel we can realistically achieve worldwide marketing, finance, and production policies." This sentiment was echoed by many other executives.

The drive for multinationalism—underscored in each MNC we studied by strong senior-management commitment—was further intensified when executives around the world agreed that the home-country orientation of the personnel function was the greatest liability to the global enterprise. This parallels the findings of two surveys commissioned by the American Management Association[1] and the Conference Board.[2] Of all the functions of the MNC, personnel was found to be the major concern of international executives. With few exceptions, efforts to make significant contributions in multinational manpower management have been short-term and unsystematic. Thus, our initial attention was on understanding and analyzing the role of the personnel function in the multinationalization process.

Designing the Measurement Program

First, key personnel decision areas, those tasks occupying the bulk of executive time, were identified. With the help of senior executives in several multinational enterprises—including IBM, Chase Manhattan Bank, W. R. Grace, SKF (Svenska Kullagerfabriken), and Caltex Oil—twenty key personnel decisions were singled out:

Manpower planning
    Forecasting personnel needs
    Job descriptions

Manpower administration
    Recruitment criteria
    Identification of prospective managers
    Screening methods
    Selection
    Assignments
        To foreign service
        To regional headquarters
        To international headquarters
        To corporate headquarters
    Development
        Performance appraisal

        Assessment criteria
        Training programs
        Promotion
        Termination
    Compensation
        Salary administration (direct)
        Other salary-related incentives (indirect)

Manpower control
    Inventory
    Audit and review

By working with MNC executives, it became possible to construct EPRG options for each key decision area. Managers were asked, "Suppose, in this decision area, a person held attitude X (say, ethnocentrism). How would he be likely to react?" These choices were then stated in a realistic fashion. Consider, for example, the decision on whom to assign to foreign service:

- *Ethnocentric:* "Prime positions in our subsidiaries are staffed with citizens of the parent country or, to a lesser extent, third-country nationals."

- *Polycentric:* "Prime positions in our subsidiaries are staffed by local nationals."

- *Regiocentric:* "Prime positions in our subsidiaries are staffed by regional citizens."

- *Geocentric:* "Nationality makes no difference in our key subsidiary positions. Competence, not passport, counts."

Next, the EPRG options were translated into questionnaire form. Respondents were asked to identify the option or options in each key decision area that best described their company's present and suggested approaches to multinational personnel management.

Although the primary research instrument was the EPRG questionnaire, other tools were also used:

1. *Personal data sheet.* To gain background information on respondents, various fact-sheet data were obtained, such as the respondent's present position, age, marital status, number of children, nationality, language proficiency, and previous overseas/headquarters experience.

2. *Advantages and disadvantages of present and suggested EPRG profiles.* Before considering changes in personnel policies, it was important to identify what MNCs might gain or lose from a significant personnel policy shift. Respondents were asked to rank the possible advantages and disadvantages of the present and suggested approaches after completing the EPRG questionnaire.

3. *Internal restraining forces and corrective measures.* A force field analysis questionnaire solicited from respondents the five most critical internal restraining forces that, in their opinion, prevented their company's becoming a truly multinational firm in the personnel area. The respondents were also asked, "What actions do you recommend be taken by your company to reduce these obstacles?"

4. *Potential objective measures to monitor multinationalization process.* Finally, respondents listed possible objective or quantitative measures on which their company's manpower management could be assessed annually in order to determine its progress in becoming more multinational.

5. *Interviews.* Approximately 35 percent of the EPRG questionnaire audience was subsequently interviewed in such diverse locations as Geneva, Honolulu, Paris, Glasgow, Genoa, New York, Grenoble, Brussels, and Newcastle.

Procedure

The total measurement package, described in the Appendix of this book, was mailed to the designated respondents in each participating company with a covering letter by senior management. Managers were then given six weeks to submit all questionnaires directly to the authors. Random interviews occurred after all written material had been received and analyzed. The diagnostic phase of the program for each firm lasted approximately five to six months; normative and structural change phases lasted up to two years.

Sample

Although several companies of various nationalities have undergone this diagnostic audit to date, we shall highlight the results we obtained in three leading MNCs—Alpha, Beta, and Gamma. Two are American, one Swedish. At the time of the program, each of these firms had annual sales in excess of $1 billion and each was one of the fifty largest firms in its country and one of the five hundred largest in the world.

Perhaps more important were the many differences among those companies sampled. Three distinct industries with widely dissimilar technologies were represented—two in diversified industrial products (Alpha and Gamma), the other in consumer packaged goods (Beta). In addition, two companies were organized along world or global lines; one maintained an international division. Further, although each firm derived at least 20 percent of its total sales revenue from foreign-based operations, the extent of international interest varied from Beta (21 percent of total) to Alpha (51 percent) to Gamma (85 percent). While Swedish Gamma had an extended history in world business (over ninety years), both Alpha and Beta were relatively new entrants, with direct overseas investment withheld until 1952. Finally, the bulk of foreign investment by Alpha and Beta was in the developed bloc of countries; Gamma's overseas network reached virtually every country of the world and was especially strong in the Third World and Eastern Europe. The people we surveyed included managers and executives in the head office and overseas. Approximately 150 people in each company—60 percent being foreign nationals—participated in this change process.

SUSPICIONS CONFIRMED

Our findings in Alpha, Beta, and Gamma confirmed the results of previous surveys. In his 1966 survey of 150 of the largest multinational enterprises, Kenneth Simmonds found that less than one percent of the senior headquarters positions were filled by foreign nationals, despite the fact that the average income generated overseas for these companies was at least 20 percent of their total income.[3] To be sure, a major limitation of the Simmonds study was its confinement to only one (though admittedly important) key decision area—assignment to corporate headquarters—but the main points are still significant.

Managers in Alpha, Beta, and Gamma chose phrases describing most of their major decision processes that reveal a low level of regional and global awareness. All three firms surveyed have heavily ethnocentric and polycentric personnel profiles (see Fig. 3.1 and Table 3.1). On the whole, the managers were troubled by this state of affairs.

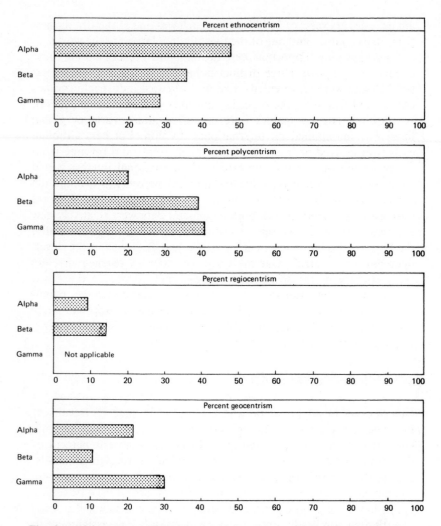

Fig. 3.1 Manpower management in Alpha, Beta, and Gamma Companies: present EPRG levels. (From David A. Heenan, *Multinational Management of Human Resources: A Systems Approach,* Austin, University of Texas, 1975, p. 53. Reprinted by permission.)

Table 3.1
Manpower Management in Alpha, Beta, and Gamma Companies: Present EPRG Levels by Company

Decision Area	Percent Ethnocentric			Percent Polycentric			Percent Regiocentric			Percent Geocentric		
	A*	B	G	A	B	G	A	B	G	A	B	G
Forecasting needs	22	11	11	13	69	56	22	33	—	44	7	33
Job descriptions	27	16	6	30	58	56	11	13	—	30	14	38
Recruitment	44	20	29	16	43	45	16	11	—	24	27	23
Prospect identification	30	34	—	11	36	—	16	16	—	38	14	—
Screening	39	13	—	17	52	—	8	18	—	35	17	—
Selection	40	18	—	28	49	—	13	19	—	17	14	—
Foreign service assignment	48	41	51	32	39	38	6	8	—	15	12	10
Regional headquarters assignment	63	54	—	12	8	—	9	14	—	7	23	—
International headquarters assignment	59	75	—	14	14	—	3	6	—	5	2	—
Corporate headquarters assignment	74	79	—	12	15	—	4	4	—	6	2	—
Assessment criteria	45	28	—	19	49	—	11	11	—	25	4	—
Performance appraisal	77	39	31	9	28	41	2	13	—	10	20	25
Training objectives	13	4	17	35	50	32	19	31	—	32	15	48
Training programs	52	16	33	23	53	35	5	16	—	20	11	29
Promotion	42	35	—	32	44	—	6	10	—	20	11	—
Termination	37	17	—	26	67	—	4	2	—	29	9	—
Salary	86	89	37	10	10	18	1	1	—	2	0	45
Incentives	56	55	33	28	40	60	4	2	—	9	4	8
Manpower inventory	40	41	31	13	14	27	4	28	—	41	17	41
Manpower audit and review	51	15	—	24	52	—	4	33	—	19	0	—
Cumulative score	47	35	28	20	39	41	8	14	—	21	11	30

Source: David A. Heenan, *Multinational Management of Human Resources: A Systems Approach* (Austin: University of Texas, 1975), p. 55. Reprinted by permission.

*A = Alpha; B = Beta; G = Gamma.

In fifteen of the twenty key personnel decision areas in the Alpha Company, ethnocentric attitudes dominated, and ethnocentrism was secondary in two others. Only the decisions regarding forecasting, job descriptions, identification, training objectives, and manpower inventory were not primarily ethnocentric. In Alpha, the most home-country-oriented decisions were compensation, performance appraisal, key assignments to headquarters (corporate, regional, and international), and salary-related incentives. On balance, ethnocentric and polycentric thinking categorized the firm's stated personnel practices.

Beta Company had a higher level of polycentrism, but less ethnocentrism than did Alpha. Twelve of its twenty personnel tasks were described primarily with phrases reflecting polycentric attitudes, and ethnocentrism dominated the other decision areas. Compensation, headquarters assignments, and salary-related incentives were the most ethnocentric, followed by assignment to foreign service, manpower inventory, and performance appraisal.

Gamma showed somewhat more polycentrism and less ethnocentrism than either Alpha or Beta. Of the ten key decision areas examined,[4] six were polycentric, three geocentric, and one ethnocentric. Ethnocentric attitudes dominated second choices.

Disadvantages of the Present Approach

Managers in all three companies pointed out the major disadvantages inherent in following their present policies. In particular, they noted that they do not use their global managers as well as they might, there are enormous communications and coordination problems, a feeling of distrust exists among the subsidiary managers, and, in general, group profits are lower than they might be. Some of their comments follow:

"With ethnocentric personnel policies, we're unable to exploit the abilities of all our high-potential candidates. Foreign nationals are essentially excluded from key slots. Under polycentrism, we miss the advantages of cross-fertilization and interchange."

"Overemphasis on either the home country or individual host countries inhibits our ability to bridge the communications gap between headquarters and overseas subsidiaries."

"By consistently relying on expatriates for key head-office and operating-company positions, the hostility of local managers is being heightened."

"Policies that encourage suboptimization restrict our ability to survive, grow, and remain profitable."

Symptoms to Watch For

It is not too difficult to compile a list of symptoms that indicate an ethnocentric attitude in the personnel area. Here are just a few that can be observed in today's MNCs:

• A disproportionately high percentage of all communications between head office and subsidiaries deals with the problems of expatriate adaptation to overseas living (for example, purchasing rugs or gaining membership in the local country club). In one MNC it represents 75 percent of the total transactions of the personnel department, two-thirds being telexes.

• The personnel officers allocate a small amount of time to counseling foreign managers about their careers compared to that devoted to counseling domestic managers about their careers. For instance, one company spends considerably more time discussing the management development opportunities of its fifty-four expatriates than it does those of its several thousand foreign nationals.

• When compared with home-country MBAs, foreign MBAs are not considered as eligible for international service. Invariably, foreign nationals are given assignments outside their home country at a much later stage in their careers.

• As a corollary, there is usually an extremely high turnover rate of foreign managers, especially those with two to seven years' service with the company.

• Foreign families coming to the United States receive relatively meager information and assistance regarding housing, education, and medical facilities. Who invites them to dinner? Who helps the family during the difficult first days?

Once these symptoms of ethnocentrism are identified and understood, every MNC may do well to conduct its own analysis and interpret the conclusions. But analysis is not the answer to a problem deeply rooted in executive attitudes.

It is understandable that, consciously or not, executives seek compatriots of similar backgrounds. Harmonious relations usually mean fewer communication problems. The chief executive officer of a large Japanese trading company feels that, although the language spoken in his company is likely to be English in about twenty years, today he would not like to risk $100 million mistakes by requiring that English be spoken. A United States executive agrees with this point of view: "It just goes easier when you can speak in your own idiom without having to explain what you mean or be careful not to say something a foreign executive might misinterpret." Similar views are held in the headquarters of French, German, and Swedish MNCs.

This kind of ethnocentrism produces a tendency for United States companies to accept those who will acculturate and become "more American than the Americans." A most surprising development is to see a non-American come to headquarters with the reputation of knowing Europe, subsequently become alienated from Europe, and ultimately accept proposals that reflect the ethnocentric orientation of headquarters.

ROOT CAUSES OF ETHNOCENTRISM

Why the lack of progress? Managers in international business argue that they are especially prone to ethnocentrism because of: (1) the immobility of non-parent-country nationals, (2) the reluctance of foreign nationals to work for managers of another culture, (3) the unique motivations of each nationality, and (4) the limited supply of competent foreign nationals. Nevertheless, our research plus that conducted by David Sirota in IBM discounts these claims.

Immobility of Foreign Nationals

Surveying approximately fourteen thousand managers of varying nationality in IBM, Sirota found that about 80 percent of the sample would like an international assignment. When asked, "Within the next five years or so, do you think you would like to have an international assignment," only 45 percent of Americans responded, "Yes, definitely." Compare this with 74 percent of Australians, 65 percent of Englishmen, 59 percent of Japanese, and 54 percent of Germans.[5] Although Latin Americans appeared somewhat disinterested in multinational careers, most foreigners were highly attracted to an international lifestyle. Generally, Americans were far less attracted to overseas opportunities than were others.

Ethnocentrism often makes it difficult for executives to assess the realities of a situation accurately. Repeatedly, head-office executives, as shown in Chapter 2, exclude subsidiary executives on the basis of their alleged immobility. There is no doubt a good deal of truth in their observations concerning foreign nationals. But, to our surprise, in one company studied we found that:

- Most of the so-called "immovables" remember no serious offer being made to them. They recall receiving hints or indirect queries, but no direct, honest discussion of making a move and its meaning.

- Most of the "immovables" could envisage jobs they would take if offered. These tended to be line, as opposed to staff, positions. They were surprised to be considered immovable!

When we relayed this information to top management, the company reconsidered its basis for selecting executives and began to include more foreign nationals in its management pool.

Reluctance to Work for Manager of Another Culture

The alleged reluctance of foreign nationals to work for a manager from a different culture was also examined. Sirota posed a series of questions—for example, "How do you think you would feel about working for an IBM manager who was from a country other than your own?" Approximately 80 percent responded that "nationality makes no difference."[6] The central finding was that there was absolutely no relationship between the nationality of managers at the top and the attitudes toward them.

Obviously there are differences between individuals and some differences between countries. But by and large, if a competent manager enters a country on an international assignment, he or she will be well received and nationality will be quite insignificant. Thus, while it is often assumed that employees resent working for a foreign manager, Sirota points out:

> In every case I have studied where a foreigner-managed subsidiary was experiencing serious difficulties, the problems stemmed not from nationality differences but rather from administrative or technical incompetence of the manager—the same kind of inadequate performance that would produce problems no matter what the nationality of the manager.[7]

In today's world, no one nationality has a monopoly on managerial competence. Indeed, subordinates are most likely to be motivated by those superiors who are capable and who can communicate their ideas effectively to senior management.

Motivational Differences of National Managers

On the issue of goal incongruence of various nationalities, another management myth was laid to rest. Sirota and Greenwood found an exceptionally high similarity of goal rankings by IBM managers around the world.[8] The average correlation of fourteen different goals (job autonomy, recognition, etc.) among the managers from twenty-seven countries was about 0.75. The greatest attractions for all managers were training and self-actualization needs. While some differences on the basis of economic and sociocultural clustering were registered, the general finding was one of overall similarities.

Unavailability of Competent Foreign Managers

Finally, consider the issue of the supposedly short supply of foreign nationals for key positions in multinational enterprises. The Conference Board identified this item as *the* critical factor restricting the international growth of multinational corporations.[9] Headquarters executives in our sample perceived the inadequate supply issue to be considerably more important than did overseas-based managers—by about a 2:1 ratio. Yet most were careful to point out that the developing countries present the greatest challenge in supplying equally competent managers. Management education in these countries, they felt, lags far behind management education in the United States, Canada, and Western Europe. Although change is taking place in some areas, managers argued that the standards are still generally below those in North America and Europe.

Executives pointed out that overseas managers usually operate in less-sophisticated business environments than that of the parent country and are often unsuited for key head-office positions. For example, one leading oil company was recently seeking a foreign national for an important regional marketing position in the United States, but only four overseas markets had credit-card systems. To transfer any manager to such a responsible domestic post without experience in credit-card systems, which are so important to petroleum marketing in North America, would have been self-defeating. As a result, an American with the appropriate credentials was promoted to the job.

There is probably some truth to the availability argument—especially when evaluating the depth of managerial talent from less-developed countries. But the argument quickly breaks down for the advanced nations, where first-rate management education and sophisticated markets have produced a substantial pool of talented managers.

When tested, the arguments of immobility, resistance to other cultures, different motivational needs, and unavailability remain unconfirmed. The fact that many executives—especially those at high levels—still perceive these forces to exist is important. And, if business enterprises are to reach the advanced stages of multinationalism, they will have to communicate the many successes of foreign nationals to those in top management.

Still, people with ethnocentric attitudes are not guilty of grievous wrong. They are simply preoccupied with one part of the world—the home country—to the exclusion of other parts. For an expanding MNC this attitude constitutes a sizable risk to its international growth.

REDUCING ETHNOCENTRISM

When Alpha, Beta, and Gamma executives were asked to identify how multinational their company's personnel function ought to be, they overwhelmingly favored less ethnocentrism and polycentrism and more regiocentrism and geocentrism. For nearly all key decision areas, geocentrism was considered the most appropriate attitude (see Fig. 3.2 and Table 3.2). In nineteen of Alpha's twenty key decision areas, geocentric attitudes were selected as best. All twenty manpower decisions in Beta were recommended for more geocentrism, and Gamma showed an almost unanimous commitment to geocentrism.

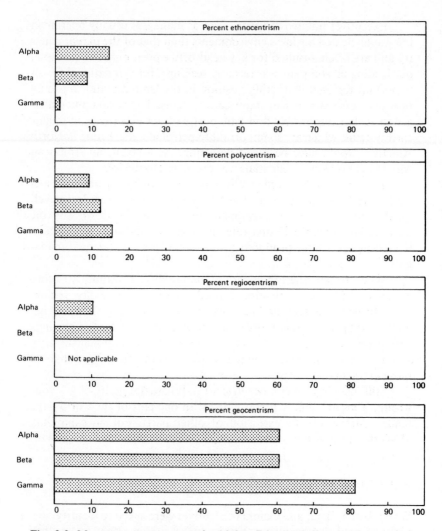

Fig. 3.2 Manpower management in Alpha, Beta, and Gamma Companies: suggested EPRG levels. (From David A. Heenan, *Multinational Management of Human Resources: A Systems Approach,* Austin, University of Texas, 1975, p. 54. Reprinted by permission.)

Table 3.2
Manpower Management in Alpha, Beta, and Gamma Companies: Suggested EPRG Levels by Company

Decision Area	Percent Ethnocentric			Percent Polycentric			Percent Regiocentric			Percent Geocentric		
	A*	B	G	A	B	G	A	B	G	A	B	G
Forecasting needs	5	0	3	8	12	20	17	37	0	69	51	74
Job descriptions	7	2	3	16	19	16	12	30	0	62	49	81
Recruitment	18	7	0	8	10	19	9	17	0	65	66	78
Prospect identification	13	14	—	4	9	—	11	17	—	68	60	—
Screening	13	9	—	7	15	—	8	7	—	65	68	—
Selection	14	4	—	15	20	—	13	18	—	52	54	—
Foreign service assignment	7	3	3	16	25	13	12	10	0	61	62	83
Regional headquarters assignment	7	2	—	6	3	—	18	27	—	59	68	—
International headquarters assignment	8	0	—	4	4	—	5	8	—	64	87	—
Corporate headquarters assignment	13	13	—	2	7	—	6	5	—	73	76	—
Assessment criteria	13	10	—	11	14	—	11	20	—	63	47	—
Performance appraisal	43	19	3	8	9	14	7	16	0	41	56	83
Training objectives	5	2	4	7	11	16	19	29	0	64	58	82
Training programs	19	4	0	8	18	16	9	19	0	60	55	81
Promotion	10	7	—	15	16	—	13	22	—	61	55	—
Termination	17	7	—	19	36	—	6	8	—	53	41	—
Salary	35	33	0	8	8	5	10	12	0	42	43	95
Incentives	14	11	3	15	13	29	9	11	0	57	66	68
Manpower inventory	8	0	0	3	2	4	5	16	0	81	82	96
Manpower audit and review	21	3	—	8	10	—	6	19	—	60	68	—
Cumulative score	14	8	2	9	13	15	10	17	0	61	61	82

Source: David A. Heenan, *Multinational Management of Human Resources: A Systems Approach* (Austin: University of Texas, 1975), p. 56. Reprinted by permission.

*A = Alpha; B = Beta; G = Gamma.

Advantages of the Multinational Approach

The most frequently mentioned advantages of a more multinational approach are better allocation of resources, a broader global outlook, improved exchange of information, and higher group profits. Individual managers said:

> "We'll have better access to the best men and ideas in the company. Today, we're missing out on good foreign nationals who are simply buried in the organization."

> "By enabling all nationalities to participate in both strategic and operational decision making, we're bound to broaden our horizons and be a more competitive force in the world economy."

> "A move away from a home- or a host-country orientation will ease informational flows between subsidiaries as well as between subsidiaries and headquarters."

> "We feel there is a strong positive relationship between medium-term group profitability and true multinationalism, because it provides greater access to resources and ideas, economies of scale, hedging against risks, improved competitiveness, and a more sophisticated corporate attitude."

These findings support the recent comments of Warren Keegan: "The trend is . . . a continuing measurable evolution in multinational corporations, toward a more geocentric mode of operation. . . . Hard-nosed businessmen now conclude that they can better achieve their maximization objectives by taking a more geocentric outlook. The reason for this is that it works."[10]

GETTING DOWN TO CRITICAL DECISIONS

An overall finding of our audit was of low present and high preferred levels of geocentrism. However, a major benefit of such an audit is its ability to isolate specific problem areas for more detailed attention and to focus on those personnel tasks that most strongly affect the evolution of the multinational firm. Our attention was on those practices that were:

- presently highly ethnocentric (or polycentric), but were singled out by respondents for more regiocentrism or geocentrism;

- perceived to be the most critical internal restraining forces in the multinationalization process;

- repeatedly identified as the major opportunity areas for improvement.

Personnel practices meeting these criteria were then categorized as *critical decision areas;* they received priority attention in the action planning sequence. Critical decision areas for all three firms were assignments to headquarters and foreign service, compensation and salary-related incentives, manpower inventory, and performance-appraisal procedures.

Assignments to Headquarters and Foreign Service

In Alpha, Beta, and Gamma, parent-country nationals have staffed the majority of key head-office and overseas posts. This central finding is probably not peculiar to these three firms. Similar results might be predicted for other leading American, European, and Japanese multinational enterprises. As Richard Lurie put it, "They all love to talk about the Brazilian in London, and the Indian in Belgium. But it is for public consumption. In private, they'll tell you that they are far from a geocentric viewpoint. Even in the companies that brag about 33 nationalities at our European headquarters, the ultimate responsibilities still lie with the American there."[11] These comments describe present-day staffing practices with a high degree of accuracy.

The true test of multinational management is what actually happens. Deeds, not words, count. Pronouncements, policies, frequent assertions of managerial beliefs in looking for competence, not passports, must be evidenced in concrete actions.

Assignment practices are considered by employees to be most important. As key stakeholders, managers tend to measure the degree of true commitment to multinationalism by who—with what nationality and competence—gets assigned where and why.

Critics of MNCs emphasize that their skepticism is reserved for those firms where outstanding talent from different countries is unknown or ignored. While key worldwide assignments are presently reserved for home-country nationals, the executives we surveyed prefer much greater utilization of nationals of that country or third-country nationals. A significant number favor polycentrism, that is, staffing local operations primarily with indigenous managers. Yet, for most managers, polycentrism is not enough. They observed that over time the polycentric approach can lead to great unevenness among affiliates and lack of minimal standards for executive talent.

Besides, leaving to local nationals the tasks of management development and succession may present considerable risks. Local managers tend to develop local fiefdoms and fail to communicate with other affiliates and with headquarters. These managers' lack of a regional or world perspective is a consequence. A more consistent allocation of the best people—irrespective of passport—is usually preferred by executives around the world.

Another form of the assignment problem can have disconcerting effects on home-country nationals as well. A natural by-product of ethnocentrism is the difficulty expatriate managers experience in reentering headquarters. Consider an actual case of a manager getting lost in orbit. Bill was sent to a Latin American country as plant manager with assurances that, from a career standpoint, this was a necessary move. Promises of future advancement seemed implicit. Anxious to return home after five years abroad, Bill found himself in a position in which his career was imperiled:

- The headquarters executive who had requested his overseas assignment and sponsored him had since left the company.

- Since he had worked primarily in a developing country, Bill was considered to be technologically obsolete.

- His former peers, who had stayed home, had been promoted into considerably bigger jobs.

- Bill was advised by the head office that the only possible opening for him would be in a remote staff department for former overseas employees, informally referred to as "the bullpen."

To deal with reentry problems, some MNCs have established a company "godfather." The title is reserved for a person of considerable stature and influence in headquarters whose role is to ensure that people on overseas assignments are neither forgotten nor allowed to neglect the growth of their functional skills. IBM has instituted such an approach; it now delegates career-planning responsibilities for officers working abroad to specific functional heads in headquarters. Other MNCs are also experimenting with this procedure.

Compensation and Salary-Related Incentives

Most corporations have extended significant overseas benefits (overseas premiums, housing allowances, home leave) to parent-country nationals on foreign-service assignments. Others working in similar positions have been compensated far less, generally in accordance with local standards. In many instances, foreigners received one-half to one-third the total compensation package of parent-company managers with identical credentials in the same job. To cite one case, an American and a third-country national were assigned to similar plant management positions in Belgium. Each man had three dependents. The third-country national, however, received only 65 percent of the housing allowance of his American counterpart. Predictably, considerable ill will resulted from this and many similar situations.

Multinational reward systems have evolved slowly. Today just a few firms maintain truly multinational compensation programs. Yet without pay practices that offer equal monetary incentives for *all* managers, companies run the risk of not attracting and retaining the high-quality professionals needed to extend their international operations.

Managerial Inventory

The manpower inventories or pools from which candidates are assigned to key overseas and headquarters positions in Alpha, Beta, and Gamma were found to be most exclusive. Only occasionally are foreign nationals included in these allegedly "worldwide" inventories, whereas parent-country managers are invariably included. Thus, one major reason for today's lack of geocentric assignment opportunities is existing management inventory practices. If the manpower pool contains only Americans, then only Americans are likely to be found in prime international positions.

Varied management inventory practices even occur within the same company. For example, in Alpha, ethnocentric, polycentric, regiocentric, and geocentric orientations are used by four different functional groups. But the company's overall philosophy encourages cross-functional mobility. Consequently, foreign nationals find top assignments possible in some functional groups (where they are included in the inventory), but not in others (where they are excluded). At best, this is disconcerting to the foreigners in the company.

On the positive side, a few firms have established geocentric man-power inventories. IBM recently formed a two-tier management pool for candidates qualified to assume the top job either in an operating company (first tier) or in world headquarters (second tier). To date, approximately two hundred candidates have been identified for each tier, with a large percentage being non-American. Several other firms are experimenting with similar programs.

Performance-Appraisal Techniques

The performance-appraisal mechanisms identified by Alpha, Beta, and Gamma managers are also ethnocentric. Parent-country tech-niques have been transferred to overseas subsidiaries with little or no variation. Foreign-based managers usually do not participate in the designing of appraisal techniques. Executives pointed out that if the procedure by which all managers are evaluated were to remain home-country oriented, foreign nationals would continue to face discrimina-tion, with key appointments reserved for citizens of the parent com-pany.

A worldwide performance-appraisal system, one that would assess managers' functional and administrative abilities plus their skills in a global setting, was proposed. Executives suggested that blending the best evaluative techniques from all over the world would enhance the total multinationalization effort.

Without question, establishing a truly multinational appraisal technique involves more than improving techniques of evaluating non-home-country personnel. An analysis of the executive biases for and against various nationalities may be in order. And, as foreigners repeat the same process of preferring their own kind, national cliques could easily form at headquarters.

To a degree, it is up to the foreign nationals to develop con-fidence to participate as equals in a home-country-dominated culture. Europeans may have to learn how to communicate more naturally with U.S. executives ("to get to the point rather than make long speeches"); they may have to develop new attitudes ("to be more posi-tive in their approach rather than constantly critical"); and they may need new behavior patterns ("to learn to argue with the boss, but know how far they can go"). Few United States headquarters execu-tives are aware of the kind of behavioral demands for conformity they are making when they Americanize their foreign executives. And, no doubt, Americans going abroad also find the acculturation process difficult.

What is most difficult to assess is the degree to which headquarters executives are evaluating the competence of the foreigner solely on the basis of learned behaviors that make that individual seem like a home-country national. ("Now, she's a good manager. She's learned to think like us!") Indeed, it will be a significant achievement for a company to establish policies and create attitudes that encourage managers to be seen for their individual merit and not for their apparent nationalities.

EXTERNAL STAKEHOLDER INFLUENCES ON KEY PERSONNEL DECISIONS

In the present environment for MNCs, the choice of key persons is increasingly influenced by the interface requirements of decision makers. As an example, one large multinational consumer products company decided on the geocentric approach to choose its country managers. All managers with good track records were to be seriously considered for more challenging positions everywhere in the world, regardless of passport.

Thus, for one key appointment, the company manager of the U.K. operation was chosen to replace the retiring head of the failing French subsidiary. The U.K. manager had an outstanding record and seemed the best person for the job. As it turned out, the main requirements of the job included negotiating in French with the French government officials and building an effective local management team. Unfortunately, the British manager spoke no French; and not understanding the "old boy" network of government officials and executives from the elite French schools, the Grandes Écoles, he found it most difficult to get things done. Consequently the French affiliate floundered, and the British manager was replaced.

This anecdote can be repeated for far too many other companies. As legitimacy criteria become more important, the requirements for senior international management is relationship-building with key stakeholders: governments, labor unions, suppliers, distributors, and other constituencies of the modern-day corporation. Nationalism demands that country management develop superior skills in communicating a profound understanding of host-country aspirations, while working within the overall corporate strategy.

As the stakeholders' expectations mount, the choice of best person for the job must relate to the position's environmental needs; and, no doubt, the legitimizing process in Western Europe, Latin America, and Asia/Pacific are probably quite different for each MNC. Hence, new conceptual skills are needed to balance company interests with stakeholder expectations such that the bargain struck is seen as reasonably fair to all parties. We would expect, for example, that personnel practices in the MNCs of the future will include the inputs of various stakeholders regarding a manager's environmental expertise.

SUMMARY

If corporate ambitions to expand a firm's international operations are to be realized, then top-level executives at home and abroad ought to be selected for and assigned to their posts with no consideration given to their nationality. Executives around the world agree that a person's competence rather than his or her passport should be the basis for promotions, privileges, and rewards, but as one senior executive put it, "It is a matter of time—of evolution, not revolution. We will need at least another fifteen years or so before we have a great variety of nationalities at corporate headquarters."

In practice, the evolutionary approach to multinationalization deals with what *ought to be*—therefore, the judgments and values of insiders. It depends on the norms of managers, the key actors in such a change process. For this reason, the starting point must be an in-depth diagnosis of organizational commitment to multinationalism. Subsequently, full and complete awareness of these value expectations underlies any process-oriented program to increase organizational effectiveness. The next chapter outlines this process in some depth.

NOTES

1. Spencer J. Hayden, "Problems of Operating Overseas: A Survey of Company Experience," *Personnel* 45, no. 1 (1968): 8–21.

2. Michael G. Duerr and James Greene, *The Problems Facing International Management,* Managing International Business, no. 1 (New York: National Industrial Conference Board, 1968), pp. 25-28.

3. Kenneth Simmonds, "Multinational? Well, Not Quite," *Columbia Journal of World Business* 1 (Fall 1966): 115.

4. At Gamma's request, only ten of the usual twenty key decision areas were audited.

5. David Sirota, "Research in International Career Planning," address to the National Foreign Trade Council, New York, April 7, 1970, p. 26.

6. Ibid., p. 28.

7. David Sirota, "The Multinational Corporation: Management Myths," *Personnel* 49 (1972): 37.

8. David Sirota and J. Michael Greenwood, "Understanding Your Overseas Work Force," *Harvard Business Review* 48 (1971): 56-59.

9. Duerr and Greene, *Problems Facing International Management,* p. 14.

10. Warren J. Keegan, Nathaniel H. Leff, David Zenoff, and Richard Lurie, "What's in the Future? New Approaches to New Realities," *Worldwide Projects and Installations* 6 (1972): 49-50.

11. Ibid.

4
A PROCESS VIEW OF GOING GLOBAL

Once there is a widely shared conviction that the benefits of true multinationalization will be substantial and the costs permissible, a con-
scious strategy of adjustment from the present to the preferred multinational profile should follow. This procedure takes time and
involves specific planning for action and a special commitment by the
chief executive officer. The first step recommended is a deliberate
attack on certain ethnocentric and polycentric attitudes. But how?

ACTION PLANNING BY CONSENSUS

There is no shortage of good ideas from both home-country and host-
country nationals on what must be done—provided discussions on this
subject are full and frank. A helpful starting point is to expose
increasingly larger numbers of managers to the multinational measurement data. Only by exposing a greater number of organizational
members to the new social norms—more geocentrism, less ethnocentrism in decision making—can major corporate recommitment be
assured. This is accomplished primarily through extensive data feedback sessions in all major organizational subunits. First, the EPRG
questionnaires are compiled and the results translated to visual form.
Next, feedback sessions are held, initially including only participants

in the Multinational Measurement Program but later extended to include all other managers. While the findings protect the confidentiality of the participating managers, they still highlight major areas of disagreement over the pace of multinationalism in the organization— for example, the differing perceptions of headquarters and operating company managers.

To cite one instance, in Alpha, initial feedback sessions on our EPRG findings included the board chairman, president, three executive vice presidents, and the vice president for personnel. Shortly thereafter, the operating council including all vice presidents in the head office was reached. Later, that same day, a presentation was also made to all department heads. Subsequently, similar sessions were held in Geneva, Brussels, and London to include all foreign nationals in positions above the department-head level. Videotapes were cut and transmitted to staff members in remote areas. Fig. 4.1 shows the flow of data feedback in the Alpha Company.

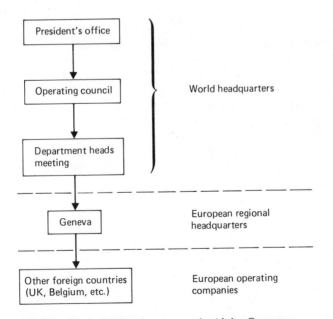

Fig. 4.1 Survey feedback sequence in Alpha Company.

In Beta, too, a worldwide managers meeting was held in Europe to induce cultural change. Survey presentations, coupled with case histories highlighting the costs of ethnocentrism, were presented. Team meetings to analyze key issues followed. During the three-day session the norms and values of the organization shifted toward more regio- and geocentrism. The type of behavior to be rewarded, how conflict was to be handled, and what was to be expected among managers of all nationalities were just a few of the value patterns that subsequently changed. Normative change in Swedish Gamma followed the same pattern.

These target-setting sessions were action oriented with a focus on the critical decision areas in manpower management. In attempting to narrow the gap between actual and desired personnel practices in Alpha Company, for example, managers developed potential objective or quantitative indices to monitor their company's efforts to multinationalize. Some are shown in Table 4.1. The dimensions, average targets, and timing to achieve these targets are presented in decreasing order of importance. For example, Alpha managers felt that the number of non-Americans assigned to key jobs was most important. An average of 18 percent of key head-office positions, they argued, should be filled by foreign nationals within nine years. A totally revamped worldwide compensation policy should be in place within three years, and so forth.

This joint target-setting process enabled senior management to sort out short-term from long-term steps to increase multinationalism. Alpha acted immediately to:

- establish a European personnel office;

- identify high-potential foreign nationals for its worldwide manpower inventory;

- develop a worldwide manpower planning activity that would facilitate international mobility;

- select several prominent citizens for its newly created International Advisory Board;

- undertake a more aggressive recruitment program aimed especially at non-Americans in United States and overseas business schools.

Table 4.1

Targets and Timing for Alpha Company's Multinationalization

Multinationalization Targets (in decreasing order of importance)	Target	Average Time Perspective (in years)
1. Number of non-Americans in		
• head office	18%	9
• overseas subsidiaries	80%	8
• parent-company board of directors	5%	8
2. Worldwide compensation policies	100%	3
3. Worldwide management training program	100%	3
4. Foreign equity participation		
• in parent company	15%	8
• in overseas subsidiaries	40%	8
5. Regional personnel office (European)	100%	1
6. International experience for key head office managers (minimum of two years abroad)	80%	15
7. Worldwide management inventory	100%	1
8. International assignments for high-potential foreign nationals	8 per annum	2
9. Multinational manpower planning process	100%	1
10. Localized research and development	25%	10
11. Language training for key head-office managers	—	2
12. International advisory groups to		
• parent company	5 members	2
• each major overseas subsidiary	5 members	5
13. Worldwide college recruitment program	100%	1

Source: Howard V. Perlmutter and David A. Heenan, "How Multinational Should Your Top Managers Be?" *Harvard Business Review*, November-December 1974, p. 131. Copyright © 1974 by the President and Fellows of Harvard College.

The firm also set up work groups to consider the longer-run issues of possible new approaches to staffing, training, compensation, and foreign equity participation.

That these targets were given priorities by company managers ensured a realistic sense of corporate commitment. In Swedish Gamma, which pioneered this research in the nine functional areas, managers' goals programs now include annual multinationalization objectives. Marketing managers, for example, must develop mutually determined quotas of new products in overseas subsidiaries. This requirement was designed to balance Gamma's worldwide product portfolio, which traditionally had been dominated by Swedish products. Other Gamma targets are shown in Table 4.2.

At first, senior management was often reluctant to solicit objective criteria—especially from "foreigners." In every company studied, these fears have been unfounded. The expectations of non-home-country nationals regarding the rate of multinationalization have always been less than those of home-country managers. Without exception, the targets established by all managers appeared quite sensible and realistically attainable.

Nevertheless, the dangers of objectives stated in terms of percentages of one nationality or another are obvious. When foreign passports become more desirable than domestic passports, reverse discrimination may result. Passport counting, geographical representation, and the like can produce negative results and even lead to tokenism. Thus, overdependence on objective indicators alone may prove risky. The underlying attitudes must be the focus—however ephemeral they may appear. And this requires senior management commitment.

SPECIAL ROLE FOR CEO

Only senior management can ensure that MNC adopts a global outlook, and the success of the change therefore depends on the commitment of the CEO. The following are typical of the many comments we received in organizations where executive management had not played an adequate role in the multinationalization process.

Table 4.2

Targets and Timing for Gamma Company's Multinationalization

Multinationalization Targets (in decreasing order of importance)	Target	Average Time Perspective (in years)
1. Relocation of corporate headquarters to neutral country	100%	1-5
2. Establishment of regional headquarters (wherever applicable)	100%	5-10
3. Foreign equity participation		
• foreign shareholders in parent company	50%	5-15
• foreign shareholders in local companies	Maximum 49%	5
• proportion of joint ventures to total Gamma investments	60-70%	5
4. Organizational decentralization; create worldwide research center, technology task force, etc.	100%	5
5. Total group exports through foreign companies	25-30%	8-10
6. Assignment to key corporate headquarters positions		
• Non-Swedes	25;50;75%	5;10;15
• Swedes	75;50;25%	5;10;15
7. Assignment to key subsidiary positions		
• Non-Swedes	80;90%	5;10
• Swedes	20;10%	5;10
8. International experience for key managers (minimum of two years abroad)	50%	10
9. Removal of individual foreign-service assignments longer than five years	100%	3
10. Personal contacts with key subsidiary managers		
• by other subsidiary managers	1 per annum	2
• by group executives	1 per annum	2
11. Multinational management inventory	100%	2
12. Multinational performance-appraisal system	100%	3-5
13. Multinational recruitment and selection program	100%	1
14. Managerial training of key non-Swedes	100%	5
15. Language training		
• English for *all* Swedish managers	100%	10
• Swedish for Non-Swedish managers	50-100%	5-10
• Local language for Swedish managers overseas	100%	2
16. Compensation		
• worldwide profit sharing	100%	5
• standard fringe benefits	100%	10
17. Geocentric task force—to ensure commitment and implementation	100%	Now

*Some Typical Comments: The CEO as an Obstacle
to Multinationalization and Recommended Corrective Actions*

Internal restraining forces	*Recommended actions*
• "Lack of *true* agreement by senior executives over the concept and practice of internationalization by our chief executive officer."	"Demonstrate corporate resolve and bring multinationalism issue into the open. Favor *true* internationalists in the hierarchy."
• "Lack of clear objectives by top management on what is to be attempted: When? Why? How measured?"	"Our chief executives should set clear, concise objectives and action plan."
• "Lack of top management commitment."	"Each functional area of the business should attempt to establish some realistic objectives or guidelines in this area."
• "Cynicism expressed by foreign managers about the president's objectives in becoming transnational."	"Our president should be able to show and demonstrate *why* this objective is desirable."
• "Lack of corporate objectives, programs, and procedures plus complete centralization at corporate headquarters."	"First things first! Define corporate policy. Set objectives. Then tackle the problems of implementation."
• "Lack of uniform understanding of our goals and objectives regarding internationalization."	"Hopefully, one result of this survey will be better identification of goals and objectives."

But this dependency, necessary as it is, causes problems. CEOs are not always at their ease in the international arena. Since most hold their top positions because of success in the domestic market, their international involvement usually comes late in their careers. For this reason, many may be tempted to ignore these issues and to overlook the home-country biases of their successors. But once begun, it is as important to maintain a multinational thrust as it is to start it in the first place.

We have often witnessed chief executives committed to multinational management concepts initiate steps to move their companies in a geocentric direction, only to have the next top-management team drop the endeavor. "We want to hear less talk about multinationalization of personnel and more about profitability. Our foreign executives have to understand that profitability is the objective, not multinationalization." Heard out of context, that incoming CEO's statement could be misinterpreted as a return to ethnocentrism; and abrupt stops and starts at senior levels can be quite damaging to managers' motivation, especially to that of foreign nationals.

Moreover, to maintain a geocentric outlook, a CEO must stay involved in a learning process. Here is some practical counsel:

• CEOs should ensure that the information they receive from their staffs is not overly biased toward the home country, and they should keep posted on all critical world events, especially those involving their major markets.

• To cultivate a genuine interest in each nation's unique role in the world economy, top management should test its own understanding of the social, political, and economic objectives of host countries.

• To minimize elements of risk and uncertainty in foreign environments, CEOs should ask themselves: "What do I personally need to know and experience so that my uncertainties in this environment are lessened?"

• Avoiding canned but comfortable presentations of the MNC subsidiaries, CEOs should visit as many markets as possible. They should beware of the whirlwind tour, which leaves them "briefed" but insulated from the realities of each country. When possible, CEOs should meet with middle managers, customers, and government officials to ask questions and listen carefully to the answers.

• CEOs should try to assess to what degree each subsidiary's management is equal to the challenges it faces. The position of top manager in an overseas subsidiary is a critical appointment. Therefore, in selecting overseas managers, the CEO should not be forced into last-minute, arbitrary choices or into playing musical chairs by rotating managers from country to country.

Legitimacy Problems and the CEO

At a recent seminar in Europe, participants included mainly company executives, government representatives, and union delegates. They were asked to imagine the following situation which might prevail in the MNCs of the late 1980s:

> Suppose you are the chief executive of a large MNC in 1990. By law you are required to include on your board of directors six different government representatives, each from a different country, with one representing the home country. Included also are union representatives from all six countries, as well as consumer advocates. The shareholders and the financial communities of the six countries are also represented. Consider some of the problems you would face in making the following key decisions: (a) launching a new product; (b) allocating R&D resources; (c) locating manufacturing facilities; and (d) promoting and rewarding senior management.

There was high consensus in the group that the situation described was likely in the future (probably in the latter part of the 1980s) and that the executives present were looking forward to retirement before such a situation arose. But, on balance, the overall reaction of the participants was one of intense disquiet. This discomfort was generated by a new awareness of how the globalization process promises unique problems of legitimacy for the MNC in a more active stakeholder environment. More specifically, executive fears were based on their expectations that:

- The six different government spokesmen would never agree, because they would only act in their self-interest.

- While the stakeholders on the board could influence what decision was taken, they would not accept responsibility for the failures as well as the successes of the firm itself.

- Only the managers themselves would have a sense of stewardship about the MNC as an ongoing organization. Others would be solely interested in running the firm down, unwittingly of course.

After considerable disagreement, some tentative consensus was reached regarding the nature of the accommodation process that will accompany the globalization of forward-looking MNCs:

1. There must be some agreed-on rules of the game. One is that, all else aside, the firm must be financially viable, if it is to retain its shareholders and maintain its standing in the financial community.

2. Some sense of balance must be found between the contribution each stakeholder makes, the capabilities of the firm, and the needs of the countries represented. Open and full discussions should underscore the process of making such trade-offs.

3. A sense of shared or joint responsibility for key outcomes must accompany any powers to influence or veto decisions.

True, these agreements were hardly unanimous. Still, they indicate how the globalization process will require learning new skills for the key actors in international business. Even assuming that the CEO is completely committed to achieving more multinationalism and that his or her senior executives are as well, several caveats regarding our suggested approach should also be considered. Some of the most important moderating influences follow.

BUILDING SEPARATE CORPORATE CULTURES

Irrespective of internal pressures to go geocentric, even within the *same* organization opinions differ over the proper EPRG profile for the firm. The level of a company's multinationality will depend on many variables, such as the potential for international business, level of technology, and sentiments of the chief executive officer. For instance, disputes may exist between managers in various functions. In Alpha Company marketing managers preferred geocentric personnel policies, while their manufacturing counterparts thought ethnocentrism best. Almost two-thirds of the marketing managers surveyed voted for a uniform global compensation policy for all high-potential managers, irrespective of nationality. Conversely, manufacturing managers elected to retain existing pay practices, with attractive incentives reserved exclusively for Americans.

These functional differences had their origins in the firm's recruitment practices. Alpha's manufacturing personnel entered from a narrow geographical base, with little or no desire to work outside the Midwest. When overseas assignments came, they were accepted reluctantly and only for brief periods. The marketing staff, on the other hand, was recruited from diverse sources and was attracted by global career opportunities. As a group they were much more committed to extended service overseas. Unable to bridge this wide cultural gap between functions, Alpha elected to design separate international compensation packages—one ethnocentric, the other geocentric—for each group.

Probably nowhere is the potential for difference over the meaning of multinationalism more intense than between overseas subsidiaries and headquarters. For various reasons—taxes, logistics, and the like—it may be desirable for MNC to take a profit in one set of overseas countries and a loss in others. For years, multinational oil companies have taken "wellhead profits" at the expense of overseas refining and marketing operations. And following the lead of the oils, MNCs in other integrated industries have insisted on maximizing the firm's profits on a global or geocentric basis for the entire firm by establishing earnings quotas for each overseas company. Necessarily, this creates conflict between those based overseas and those in corporate headquarters.

Local owners and managers, even when informed of the rationale for not taking a profit in their country, are quite insensitive to the problem. Quite understandably, their attention is on maximizing the performance of local operations, or polycentrism. But those in headquarters argue that they alone have the global perspective needed to optimize the company's total resources. Inevitably, conflicts erupt, and only one solution is fail-safe: experiential learning in another culture. After only two years in an overseas subsidiary, managers assigned from headquarters have almost identical expectations and values as local managers.[3] And for foreign nationals, a tour of duty in the head office has the same effect. Cross-learning of this variety provides foreign nationals with the institutional picture and sensitizes home-country nationals to the needs of each country operation.

Who is "foreign" in a worldwide company? Or, what is "domestic"? As a company expands internationally, the "home country" is not home for more and more executives. These handy, but inaccurate, labels lead to the blatant mismanagement of people. Further, the constant reference to "home" versus "abroad" reveals a deep-seated ambivalence about multinationalization in today's MNCs. Such ambivalence necessarily influences intraorganizational consensus on which version of multinationalism is best for the firm.

Thus, the EPRG profile of a firm varies by product, function, and geography. And there may not even be consensus within the same company on the ideal form of multinationalism. Care should be taken to identify appropriate areas for policy differentiation. Attempts to generalize any one particular multinational profile and strategy onto a diverse internal audience are of limited value.

BEYOND THE PERSONNEL FUNCTION

Recall, too, that the intervention point for most OD efforts has been the personnel function. Multinationalizing the human factor, it was felt, must precede all other functional applications. Yet all too familiar is the tokenism associated with the management of human resources. And, as our findings indicate, probably nowhere is this lip service more visible than in the international dimension.

For firms in many industries, the importance of the personnel function is probably overstated. With the notable exception of some segments of the service industry—management consulting, public accounting, financial services, and a few other areas—MNCs can survive quite nicely with an average, but stable, work force. Access to raw materials, technology, market intelligence, and financial resources may outweigh the need for truly exceptional managers in large numbers. Competition in most industries is based primarily on business functions other than personnel. Or, as one senior executive pointed out, "While personnel is an important area to consider, we're predominantly a marketing-oriented company. To make any significant headway [here], we'll need a similar investigation in the *marketing* function. Eventually, we probably should also include finance and production." Therefore, any serious MOD program must be multifunctional as well as multinational.

Responding to these realities, parallel attempts have been initiated to analyze multinationalism in the marketing, finance, and operations functions.[4] By examining numerous corporate decisions, ranging from pricing to inventory control, progress has been made beyond the personnel function. Some of the preliminary findings are:

1. *Marketing practices* are described as now being highly polycentric. For most decision areas, this high level of local sensitivity is considered most desirable. The exceptions are product design and quality, branding, and sales administration, where geocentrism is preferred.

2. *Operations or production decisions* are perceived to be even more localized or polycentric than marketing. But here there is some dissatisfaction as managers generally prefer a more regiocentric or geocentric approach to the function.

3. Today's *financial decisions* are either ethnocentric or polycentric. The overall preference is for geocentrism, especially for those decisions relating to investment criteria, stock listing of the parent company, overseas investment profile, and profit standards.

While these results have been useful in building a broader base of corporate consensus to multinationalize, all is not perfect. The non-personnel dimensions—particularly financial management—are influenced to a large extent by variables outside the control of the firm. Flexible exchange rates, interest equalization taxes, and different accounting and taxation systems are just a few of the environmental factors that reduce the validity of an attitudinal audit of other business functions.

For example, United States subsidiaries operating overseas are now following a policy of remitting earnings to the parent country rather than reinvesting those earnings locally or redeploying them on a regional or global basis. On first blush this seems like ethnocentrism. In fact, it is not. Present United States investment restraints require direct remission of the foreign-source income of American companies to the United States *prior* to geographical redistribution (after taxes). This makes it most difficult to assess accurately the true multinational profile of the firm.

Alternatively, the Swiss subsidiary of a United States MNC may follow a policy of borrowing locally rather than in parent-country, regional, or worldwide money markets. On the surface, this seems to reflect polycentrism; but, under closer scrutiny, something else is taking place. Swiss lending rates may simply be much lower than those in all other countries. By borrowing locally in Swiss francs, the profit-oriented treasurer is minimizing the cost of capital to the Swiss company at that particular point in time. Tomorrow, if interest rates were to increase, the treasurer would seek out funds from alternative money markets. The initial decision to borrow locally for the local subsidiary in Switzerland may not have been polycentric, but rather geocentric (since it represented the best source of funds in the world at that time).

These different courses of action were influenced primarily by the inherent risk factors of borrowing, not by any general attitude toward multinationality. To understand corporate multinationalism in the decades ahead, new technologies, beyond the personnel function, must be developed.

THE INADEQUACIES OF INTROSPECTION

Institution building does not take place in a vacuum, and the relationship of any multinational corporation to the world outside is critical. Moreover, environmental pressures on the MNCs of today and tomorrow are on the rise. As indicated earlier, other countervailing forces are undergoing their own evolution toward multinationalism.

Take, for example, the challenge of multinational unionism. True, national customs and laws make it extremely difficult for a national union to recruit members in a foreign country and win the right to represent them in collective bargaining. But, increasingly, national unions are participating in multinational coalitions, and this kind of international cooperation should be taken seriously.

The most active multinational labor organizations are the International Confederation of Free Trade Unions and the International Trade Secretariats. While the former links national union blocs such as the Canadian Labour Congress and the British Trades Union Congress, the latter are groupings of individual unions by trade or industry. And, on balance, the clout is with the International Trade Secretariats. The International Metalworkers Federation, for instance, claims 11.5 million members in sixty countries; the International Transport Workers Federation operate in eighty nations with 6.5 million workers; and so on.

With strength of this order, multinational unionism must be analyzed carefully. In 1972 the International Federation of Air Line Pilots Association successfully undertook the world's first multinational, multicompany shutdown—in response to governments' failure to take action against airline hijackers. Less dramatic, but equally effective, efforts have been recorded. The emerging pattern is clear: collective bargaining, coordinated on a regional or global basis, is on the way.

Thus, if MNCs of tomorrow are to survive and prosper, their managements must understand and cope with the emerging network of labor unions, governments at home and abroad, consumer groups, and others. These external forces will exert a significant influence in shaping the multinational profile of future corporations.

THE LIMITS OF GEOCENTRISM

Finally, it would also be a mistake to assume that geocentrism is desirable or inevitable for all companies in the world. Frequently, companies enjoy a strong position in the domestic market and a record of failure overseas. For most companies about to leap into irreversible commitments abroad, it is advisable to conduct a thorough analysis of staying at home before plunging headlong into the international scene. And, for many firms, ethnocentrism in many decision areas may be a *desirable* course for the next several years. Such a determination, however, should only be made after seriously considering the advantages and disadvantages of ethnocentrism.

Indeed, nowadays there is a noticeable upswing in reverse investment—that is, returning home—especially for American MNCs. After generating almost three decades of economic challenge overseas, many United States multinationals have become recommitted to the home market. Some observers of the international business scene attribute this pullback to the American market to the rising superiority of European and Japanese competition.[5] And "the non-American revenge," as it has become known, has caused many American MNCs to reconsider the wisdom of their precipitate plans for international growth.

In no small part, the rising attractiveness of the United States market has caused this reversal. Several factors are responsible:

1. *Improved competitiveness of the American worker.*   The relative tranquility of United States unions—reflected in extended strike-free periods, rising productivity, and realistic wage demands—reestablished American labor on at least an equal (if not better) footing as its counterparts in Western Europe. In recent years, labor costs in the United States have been rising much more slowly than in most other industrial countries. Consider these comparisons of hourly compensation, which is a close proxy for labor costs.

In 1970, the U.S. level of compensation was in a position of lonely eminence, with only Canada approaching it. But by midyear 1975, hourly compensation in Canada and West Germany had risen to parity with the United States. Belgium's level was higher, and Sweden's even higher still. In several other industrialized countries, the gap between the United States level had dwindled, with Britain the sole exception to this general trend.

Moreover, the importance of labor costs should not be understated. By some measures, employee compensation accounts for about 75 percent of the value added in the manufacturing sector in the United States, 70 percent in Western Europe, and 50 percent in Japan. Hence, the international convergence of average compensation in recent years has served as a powerful driving force in motivating American and non-American investors to reexamine the newly enhanced attractiveness of the United States as a manufacturing base.

2. *Relative strength of the United States economy.* Quite similarly, the inflationary effects of the American market, while much discussed at home, were considerably less than those being experienced elsewhere around the world. The relative size and diversity of the United States economy also seemed more able to ride out the shocks of oil and other raw-material restrictions that characterized recent years. Compared with Japan, Western Europe, and the developing countries, the economic appeal of the United States recaptured the eye of investors. This rekindled interest in the United States market was, of course, not restricted to American MNCs. Shared by firms of other nationalities, it was reflected in an average annual upswing of 20 percent in foreign direct investment in the United States over the last four years.

3. *Closer access to resources.* As a corollary, extremely tight money conditions existed in Western Europe and Japan. But American firms found it easier to meet their financial needs on Wall street. The relative ease with which prime borrowers could acquire local capital also influenced their decision to invest at home.

4. *Rise in political uncertainty overseas.* The post-Vietnam period and the subsequent withdrawal of U.S. military forces from Southeast Asia created an atmosphere of heightened political and economic uncertainty in the Pacific Basin. While bystanders waited to examine the economic effects of falling dominoes, United States multinationals

were hesitant to commit additional resources to the area. Many swung their attention back to the domestic market. Further, the evaporation of Beirut as the hub of the Middle East, continued strife in Argentina, and the collapse of democratic conditions in Italy all typified the kinds of political exposure that confronted American businesses in the 1970s. Even in supposedly friendly countries—Canada, Australia, and Japan—United States multinationals, for the first time, were being singled out for attack. These factors and more caused many U.S.-based MNCs to reemphasize the home market at the expense of international growth. To a degree, geocentrism was put on the back burner in the boardrooms of the American and European multinationals.

For Japan, too, somewhat different considerations made its MNCs reevaluate the direction and thrust of their overseas expansion plans. The price to be paid for achieving economic dominance in Southeast Asia was all too visible to the nation as it viewed on television the rude reception that Prime Minister Tanaka received from Thai students in 1972. These demonstrations and other incidents that followed in several Southeast Asian countries forced Japanese executives from both the private and public sector to alter their country's economic policies. Today, Japan maintains a much lower profile in the developing countries of Asia, with a reallocation of resources to the home market and the developed countries of the West.

What are the implications? Today, more than ever before, MNCs are reassessing most carefully the nature of their commitment to geocentrism. In keeping with our discussion in Chapter 1 of the current changes in the global industrial system, the overly ambitious plans to establish a far-flung network of international operations are being modified to meet the realities of the times. While still the theme of banquet speeches by CEOs around the world, geocentrism is considered by many to be conceptually interesting but perhaps operationally unmanageable—at least in the short run.

CHANGING CONCEPTS OF GEOCENTRISM

As nationalist and subnationalist sentiments grow in both the advanced and developing countries, and as the value system of the stakeholders changes from elitist to egalitarian concerns for the basic needs for health, education, housing, a safe environment, and food, top management is being forced to question the premises on which their geocentric strategies are based. The viability and the legitimacy of the following factors seem especially vulnerable:

- MNCs' setting of financial and marketing objectives that do not relate to the social and economic priorities of the countries in which they operate;

- the development of products and services primarily directed at customers in the more affluent enclaves of those countries;

- the encouragement of capital-intensive technology, often beyond the reach of most users;

- dogmatic policy of wholly owned subsidiaries in all parts of the world;

- the exclusive investment in management development of those whose primary capabilities are in the traditional business functions: marketing, finance, and production.

We call this syndrome geocentrism of the *enclave* variety, because the enterprise's activities are only marginally related to the high-priority problems of the nations in which they operate.[6] By the same token, managers representing the MNC often live in urban enclaves or "golden ghettos," with little sensitivity to the human needs of the popular majority. This is true in both developed and developing countries.

Consequently, a new meaning of geocentrism is emerging. It is based on a quite different understanding of conditions under which the viability and legitimacy of the firm must be based. *Integrative* geocentrism recognizes that a MNC's key decisions must be separately assessed for their impact on each country.

To illustrate the integrative-geocentric approach, consider the following policy implications:

- Goal setting in both the home and host country with a primary concern for their social and economic priorities, particularly employment.

- The development of marketing policies—product design, pricing, channels of distribution—aimed at larger segments of the population, including the less affluent.

- The encouragement of a spectrum of technologies, including those that utilize indigenous resources to a fuller degree. (For instance, less energy-intensive processes are designed for energy-poor countries.)

• The creation of a portfolio of ownership patterns including licensing, joint ventures, technical assistance, and management contracts, as well as 100 percent ownership (where proprietary technology is involved). The ultimate choice considers the country's basic infrastructure needs.

• The long-term commitment to upgrading skilled managers outside the traditional business functions.

• As a corollary, the developing of managers whose capabilities include the identification of the needs and priorities of the countries in which they live, and whose skills can improve the human condition of these countries.

An illustration of the integrative-geocentric orientation in a developing country is found in Chapter 7. In our view, this approach will become the watchword for all countries, since all countries, to some measure, are "developing."

SUMMARY

To narrow the gap between where a multinational is and where it wants to be requires full-scale commitment involving senior management's stamp of approval and involvement. The process must start at the top—and then move downward into the lifeblood of the organization.

An internationally oriented OD program is not restricted in its use of technology. Nor is it defined by the technology that it employs. In the main, the tools and techniques discussed in this chapter were developed within the context of each enterprise. As such, these tools were frequently used to meet specific objectives: a more balanced product portfolio, a more efficient communications network, or a more equitable worldwide compensation system. The range of techniques that can be applied is infinite. For instance, in the entry stages, the EPRG analysis played a key role, but also used were:

• diagnostic reviews of correspondence between headquarters and overseas companies;

• demonstration projections, with key program participants attending relevant joint sessions, to reinforce felt needs;

- confrontation meetings between disaffected subunits within the firm.

No doubt there are multiple variations of these themes. And, in years to come, the most innovative applications of process consultation will occur in the international dimension.

Moreover, pressures from within and outside worldwide companies will determine the proper multinational heading for the firm.[7] In most instances, a full-scale drive towards geocentrism is unrealistic in the short term. For many MNCs, regionalism provides the answer, and the next chapter discusses OD at the regional level.

NOTES

1. For other functional applications, see David A. Heenan, "The Role of the Personnel Function in the Multinationalization Process of Worldwide Institutions," Ph.D. dissertation, University of Pennsylvania, 1972. For a more complete discussion of the EPRG approach to marketing, see Yoran Wind, Susan P. Douglas, and Howard V. Perlmutter, "Guidelines for Developing International Marketing Strategies," *Journal of Marketing* 37 (April 1973): 14-23.

2. For a description of the rising multinationalism in trade unions, see David C. Hershfield, "The Challenge of the Multinational Union," *The Conference Board Record* (December 1974), p. 11. For a contrary opinion, see Herbert R. Northrup and Richard L. Rowan, "Multinational Union Activity in the 1976 U.S. Rubber Tire Strike," *Sloan Management Review* (Spring 1977): 17-28.

3. David A. Heenan, *Multinational Management of Human Resources: A systems approach* (Austin Texas: University of Texas Bureau of Business Research, 1975), pp. 57-60.

4. Sanford Rose, "Why the Multinational Tide is Ebbing," *Fortune,* August 1977, pp. 111-120.

5. Ibid.

6. Howard V. Perlmutter, "Two Concepts of Geocentrism: Enclave and Integrative," Working Paper, The Wharton School, University of Pennsylvania, 1978.

7. "The Coming Transformation of the TNC," *Report of the World Economy Research Project,* Worldwide Institutions Group, The Wharton School, University of Pennsylvania, 1978.

5
REGIONAL ORGANIZATION DEVELOPMENT

Some managers argue that the multinational target-setting approach is not the best option, given the relative remoteness of geocentric management concepts. They suggest that a more realistic and timely option is regiocentrism. Through regional organizational forms and managerial processes, a not-quite-global perspective can be gained without sacrificing management control and effectiveness.[1]

For years, corporate planners groped with the proper role and organizational fit of the regional headquarters. Arguing against regional offices was the long-standing dual criteria for a successful worldwide organizational structure[2]:

1. *Strategic planning and control must be centralized*, presumably at corporate headquarters located in New York, Tokyo, or some other central location.

2. *Local planning and operations must be decentralized,* at the host country or subsidiary level.

No consideration was given to an intermediate structural concept at the regional level. Consequently, many questions regarding the regional headquarters emerged: Would it engage in the firm's strategic issues, such as pricing, foreign equity participation, and offshore financing? Would it share with overseas subsidiaries in operational decisions for, say, hiring and firing, facilities management, and other day-to-day issues, or would some combination of strategic and operational decision making be undertaken by the regional organization? In large part, the answers to these questions did not come easy for all companies.

Nevertheless, since the mid-1960s, a noticeable trend in American, European, and Japanese MNCs has been integration of their overseas operations on a geographic or regional basis. Aided by institutions like the European Economic Community and the Eurodollar Market, regionalism is now commonplace. Today, two out of every three American MNCs have some form of regional organization, complete with headquarters; this is true for British, Swedish, German, and French companies as well. Even companies with such diverse needs as Exxon, Ford, ICI, and SONY have gone the regional route.

SIGNIFICANT DRIVING FORCES

Several factors are most often cited by executives as the primary incentives for going regional:

1. *Reduced span of control.*   The tremendous growth and expansion of international business since the 1950s is well recorded. Take, as one example, Citibank of New York. In 1962, it had offices in less than thirty countries; today, it has over 1,000 offices in 103 countries. To monitor such a far-flung international network, which contributes over two-thirds of total corporate earnings, on a country-by-country basis is simply not feasible. Regional reporting of foreign subsidiaries provides the answer. For Citibank, this takes the form of three regional and several subregional (or area) headquarters.

2. *Greater area sensitivity.*   With a physical presence in a region, a MNC is assured of improved awareness of environmental and market conditions. Whether it is dealing with regional institutions like the Asian Development Bank or the Central American Common Market, the company with a regional capability is in a much better position to respond to area needs. Access to financial intermediaries, competitive information, and government and related agencies offers added incentive for the firm to organize closer to its primary overseas markets.

3. *Better allocation of resources.*   Global firms also experience major advantages in regional resource allocation. From a plant in north-

ern Germany, General Foods supplies its entire European network with freeze-dried coffee. Nice, France serves as the base for IBM's regional "center of competence" in research and development. Caterpillar Tractor's European marketing campaign is directed from its Geneva headquarters. Such examples are illustrative of the numerous instances where worldwide companies are experiencing significant economies of scale through regionalism. As corporate activities are so clustered, executives see the need to make all key business decisions on a similar basis. They argue that it takes a regional organization—preferably one based in the field—to oversee resource allocation.

4. *Intense competition for talent.*   Today's high-potential candidates, especially those in Europe, are seeking diverse career opportunities. One of the major attractions of the United States multinational to the talented European is the possibility of a career in several countries. But recently, when a recruiter for an American chemical company proudly announced to a potential German candidate at INSEAD that "the managing directors of all of our European subsidiaries are local nationals," he was surprised that the student was totally unimpressed. "If," replied the student, "I wanted to spend my career in Germany becoming managing director of a chemical company, I would not be talking to you but to BASF or Bayer. At least in *these* companies, I know my progress would not be blocked by Americans." Thus, whereas the top slots in their local subsidiaries may have previously satisfied most European MBAs, many are now pressing for relatively immediate assignments elsewhere in Europe and the rest of the world. Very few American firms have successfully met these demands.

Nor has this challenge been confined solely to foreign nationals. Younger American managers, particularly those in the financial services industry, are now being seriously wooed by European, Brazilian, and other companies for the first time. For example, one American banker on assignment to Italy recently accepted a major position with an Italian investment bank for a 200-percent increase in salary. No longer can MNCs expect career dedication to the homeland of the parent company.

These phenomena will pose an increasingly serious threat to all companies with global interests. An effective response can be made through the regional organizations by providing attractive career paths for managers of all nationalities.

5. *Need for managerial conduit.*   As a corollary, many foreign nationals find that the top positions in their home countries often go to those with headquarters exposure and, hence, institutional visibility as well as a line track record in another country. On the basis of extensive personnel research, IBM made both experiences prerequisite to a manager's assuming command of his or her local susidiary. For several companies, regional headquarters serve as the appropriate vehicle through which local managers can ascend the corporate hierarchy.

Firms that have organized along regional lines clearly outperform others in the development of foreign nationals.[3] Typically, 40 to 70 percent of the key executives in regional headquarters are nationals of countries in the area; the remainder are from the parent country. Local participation is especially high if the area headquarters is located within the region. By encouraging the interaction of executives of different nationalities, the regional headquarters may ease the transition to a geocentric management team in corporate headquarters.

6. *Unbalanced training programs.*   Several companies have experienced an unevenness across national boundaries in their training and management development programs. Several years ago, for example, overseas training took place in some Citibank locations and was excellent; in others, either nothing existed or it was poorly done. As a result, the bank consolidated its training into several regional centers (Milan, London, and Manila) and so assured divisional standards. For some firms, regional companies have been almost exclusively established to service this need.

CRITICAL FACTORS FOR SUCCESS

While there are important incentives to regionalize key managerial decisions, each firm should ensure that the following essential ingredients are present.

1. *Executive commitment.*   For regional headquarters to succeed, all levels of management—head office, regional, and subsidiary—must be behind regional-headquarters personnel and be willing to give them the resources needed to do their jobs effectively. Those concerned must have their hearts in it!

In determining their true sense of commitment to, say, regional management, host-country heads should ask themselves: Would I be willing to close or scale down my local training activity for an improved regional center? Would I nominate a key manager who's in great need of a regional assignment just to improve his or her career? Would I accept a manager for an important position here simply on the recommendation of a regional executive?

Similar questions should be asked of other managers. For example: Will the parent-country staff perceive these programs as a form of "reverse discrimination"? This very result has accompanied some programs, with unfortunate consequences.

2. *Regional integrity and balance.* For geographic management approaches to be viable, operational planning must be integrated on a regional basis. Premature attempts to establish full-fledged regional headquarters in areas not yet ripe for truly regional factor mobility—as, for example, the Andean Common Market—will be futile. For most firms, this probably means that Europe may be the primary locus of regionalism in the seventies and eighties.

Regional companies must also be truly regional in character and staffing. They should not be extensions of one nationality over others in the region. For example, if the regional director is Dutch, it may be desirable to balance the staff with, say, competent Germans and Italians. As a sign of the times, few managers, if any, will accept the idea that any one nationality has a monopoly on managerial knowledge.

Moreover, regional integrity without balance has its costs. Regional chauvinism can threaten the headquarters' effectiveness and very existence. Overidentification with the area organization inhibits institutional awareness and leads to corporate suboptimization. In a typical case, managers may find their career opportunities restricted to one geographical area. Or, interchange of information on, say, new approaches to sales training may be blocked from other regions.

Regional myopia usually can be avoided through combined OD efforts at the corporate and regional level. These joint approaches, discussed later in the text, can best ensure that people, resources, and ideas are exchanged on a worldwide basis.

3. *Realistic mandate.* Regional headquarters should not lose sight of reality. There is a strong tendency to forget objectives. Such comments as, "All we need now for a successful program is an Albanian in London," are all too common. Private corporations need not emulate the United Nations.

Firms should be sensitive to the number of high-potential foreign nationals who merit regional assignments and should establish a reasonable timetable for these transfers. Regionalization is usually an elite process, focusing on those especially talented persons who are also more mobile. Thus, MNCs should not create an atmosphere that forces local managers with neither regional ability nor mobility to work abroad. Local nationals provide the operational continuity for the firm in their home countries. Attractive and meaningful *domestic* career paths for these individuals must also be developed.

But beware of overkill. Some of the most successful regional efforts have been task oriented, designed to self-destruct after completion of rather specific, limited objectives. Special ad hoc programs to reduce the number of expatriates in Latin America or to make a major acquisition in Europe are two recent examples of relatively narrow, yet effective, approaches to area organization. In both cases the organization was deactivated within two years. For many firms, contingent organizational strategies may be most appropriate.

4. *Proper intraorganizational relations.*   Vital to the success of the regional office are appropriate reporting relations for its key staff functions—marketing, finance, operations, personnel, and others. Regional staff executives, such as the director of European marketing, may report directly either to the senior regional line executive or to their senior functional counterparts at corporate or international headquarters. The final choice depends on how the region is organized.

If the area has true profit-center responsibilities, a strong case can be made for directly reporting to corporate line management. To divorce key staff activities from the staff's line users invites disaster. Unresponsiveness on the part of the head office in terms of needed guidance and approval is a frequent criticism. Without control over staff activities, line managers tend to adopt a do-it-yourself attitude and slowly absorb many decisions themselves. By isolating them from the line, MNCs can expect weak, dysfunctional relationships in the region.

However, the situation is somewhat different if the regional office is actually a "paper tiger"—without profit and loss responsibility, or with profit-center responsibility but encouraged to "rely exclusively on our excellent services back in corporate headquarters." Here, staff executives can gain strength from a straight line relationship with their head-office superiors. Where the rationale for the area organization is simply one of organizational convenience, a strong self-identity for staff functions is most desirable. The line's needs are somewhat less intense and, in a sense, less legitimate. Regionally based officers have a clear need to consult headquarters for overall direction and operational assistance. Open and direct lines of communication are needed. This is best ensured by the regional staff's reporting directly to a corporate or international-division staff executive.

Even then, however, the regional headquarters may have a short life span. Consider, for example, the case of a large American multinational that established a regional headquarters in Europe. The mission of the regional office was to develop a regional strategy in marketing and production, and to rationalize the activities of the various operating countries. But, after two years, and with very little advance notice, the office was reduced from 120 to 3 individuals.

The failure of this area headquarters contains some instructive lessons. Before the regional office was created, the CEO had direct contact with country managers and had developed a personal relationship with them. Once the regional structure was established, however, his access to this group was diverted. Naturally, the country managers also preferred to deal directly with the CEO, for he could make decisions on the spot. In addition, the international headquarters and corporate staffs saw the area headquarters as an obstacle to getting their ideas into the countries.

Then there was the problem of heavy expenses. Operating units were charged overhead costs of the regional headquarters. Since the regional office seemed to contribute little in terms of improved country performance, country managers naturally viewed these overheads as unjustified and unnecessary.

Perhaps most important, country managers were not committed to the management development of personnel on the regional staff. Rather, their rewards were for country performance, and losing good people to the regional headquarters was not considered in the interests of the country management.

"They are not helpers; they are nuisances!" was the perception of the country managers. "They act as a barrier rather than a conduit of our ideas," complained corporate and international managers. In short, the regional structure lost its legitimacy as well as its supporters, including the CEO. The result was predictable.

In today's complex environment, there are strong stakeholder pressures to remain polycentric. For this particular firm, the regional approach lost sight of host-country needs and failed to balance local interests with those of the larger organizational domain.

5. *First-team staffing.* Top-quality management is essential in regional headquarters. Yet major corporations frequently fail to adequately staff this important activity. For example, only about one-third of the Americans working abroad as regional personnel executives in United States multinationals have had any previous overseas experience. Alternatively, regional staffing is left to the local subsidiaries. In many instances, young and inexperienced personnel form the ranks of the area headquarters. We have often heard the complaint that, rather than helping the operating companies, members of the regional staff "are running around to get information from one subsidiary to claim as their own, and then tell another subsidiary what to do." Far too often, regional companies are staffed by those who could not make the grade elsewhere.

Hence, regional executives must be careful to build the quality involvement of managers in the operating subsidiaries. Their collaboration is invaluable. MNCs successful in their attempts at regionalism are able to tap these local resources effectively.

BUT TRUST MUST BE EARNED

For the regional headquarters to be perceived as indispensable and legitimate, a sense of esprit must be instilled in regional personnel. Selected OD techniques, in particular team building, can be especially helpful here. Consider a few recent examples of successful collaborative approaches.

1. *The regional task force.* When a European personnel office was established in Brussels a few years ago by General Foods, it was intentionally given only a skeletal staff, thereby forcing reliance on local personnel units. A European Personnel Managers Task Force, consisting of regional and country personnel managers, was formed. With their line management's consent, the local representatives received periodic regional assignments based on their respective areas of expertise. For example, the British personnel-office manager, an acknowl-

edged compensation specialist, was assigned regional benefits projects; his French counterpart had regional management-development responsibility; and so on.

The task force met bimonthly to discuss common problems and possible solutions. Managers reported back the results of their special assignments. State-of-the-art sessions were also conducted by designated team members. Over a relatively short time, a wide range of personnel subjects was covered by the group, and the professional caliber of local personnel staffs was distinctly improved. But most important, the participative style of the task force fostered a strong sense of regional identity among personnel officers. Eventually, other staff functions launched similar programs.

2. *Regional seminars.* Another leading company adopted mini-seminars as a vehicle for interchanging ideas and developing regional cohesiveness. In one such seminar the marketing managers of the major European subsidiaries were brought together with sixteen high-potential candidates from other functional areas. By affording younger managers regional visibility, this approach eventually encouraged a high degree of cross-functional as well as cross-national mobility.

3. *The regional audit.* To involve more fully its local financial managers in regional management, a major European company established a rotational audit and review system. On a quarterly basis, several problem areas, such as foreign-exchange management and inflation accounting, were examined by a joint headquarters-subsidiary team. A representative from regional headquarters would then travel, say, to the British subsidiary and review that company's performance in these areas. The approach was essentially educational, and criticism was constructive. When finished, the regional financial manager, joined by his British counterpart, would proceed to Belgium. While there, the local company would undergo a similar financial audit. But here, the British manager would assume primary responsibility. Next, the Belgian officer would analyze the Dutch subsidiary, and so on throughout Europe. After several such audits, local financial managers better understood the strategic needs and informational requests of regional headquarters. As with the task force, this approach spread to other staff functions within the company.

4. *Rotational assignments.* In another well-known firm, local officers are often assigned to the regional staff as a step to assuming

the top jobs in their home countries. These broadening assignments also fill critical staffing needs in the area. Other MNCs encourage short-term developmental tours of duty in third countries within the region. A few rotate talented line officers through regional and country staff functions with excellent results.

REGIONAL COALITION STRATEGIES

Besides traditional forms of regionalism, a related trend in MNCs toward *multiple* national identities will demand even more innovative approaches to organization development.[4] With European company statutes now encouraging conglomeration, we call these coalitions "Global Industrial Systems Constellations" (GISCs) to distinguish them from a single firm managed from a single corporate headquarters where the strategy is global. Figure 5.1 shows a listing of such coalitions for the period 1900 to 1972. But recently, too, marriages of worldwide companies beyond the simple joint venture variety are being consummated at an accelerating rate. Some, visible today, include:

- the Italian Banco de Roma, the French Credit Lyonnais, and the German Commerzbank agreement to offer regional financial services;

- the merger of Bulova Watch and Hong Kong-based Stelux Manufacturing to market and manufacture watches on a worldwide basis;

- the joint agreement between Japan's Kawasaki Steel Corporation, Italy's Societa Finanziara Siderugia, and Brazil's Siderugia Brasileira to develop an integrated steel plant and deep-water harbor facilities in Brazil.

Nor are these corporate coalitions confined to the developed world. Other nations also view them as effective means to regionalize, and among some of the more interesting current examples are:

- *The evolution of OPEC multinationals.* Today the Triad Holding Corporation, based in Lebanon, stands as the first Arab-owned-and-managed conglomerate. With assets of $400 million, its investments include oil tankers in Indonesia, cattle-feeding operations in Brazil, and fashion houses in France.

Year	Merger Partners	Country	Surviving Company
1907	Royal Dutch Petroleum	Netherlands	Royal Dutch Shell
	Shell Transport and Trading	Great Britain	
1930	Lever Brothers	Great Britain	Unilever
	Margarine Union	Great Britain	
	Margarine Unie	Netherlands	
1951	AB Aerotransport	Sweden	Scandinavian Airlines System (SAS)
	Det Danske Luftfartselskab A/S	Denmark	
	Det Norske Luftfartselskab A/S	Norway	
1962	Deutsche Grammophon (subsidiary of Siemens)	West Germany	Polygram
	Philips Phonographic Industries (subsidiary of Philips)	Netherlands	
1964	Agfa	West Germany	Agfa-Gevaert
	Gevaert	Belgium	
1969	Enka (subsidiary of AKU)	Netherlands	Enka-Glanzstoff (subsidiary of Akzo)
	Glanzstoff (subsidiary of AKU)	West Germany	
1969	N.V. Koninklijke Nederlandse Vliegtuigenfabriek Fokker	Netherlands	Fokker-VFW
	Vereinigte Flugtechnische Werke	West Germany	
1971	Dunlop	Great Britain	Dunlop-Pirelli
	Pirelli	Italy	
1971	Schmalbach-Lubeca Werke	West Germany	Europembailage (subsidiary of Continental Can Co.)
	Thomasson en Drijver	Netherlands	
1972	Douwe Egberts	Netherlands	Douwe Egberts-Jacobs
	Jacobs	West Germany	
1972	Hoesch	West Germany	ESTEL
	Hoogovens	Netherlands	

Source: *McKinsey Quarterly*, 1974.

Fig. 5.1 Global industrial systems constellations, 1900–1972.

- *Latin-owned multinationals.* Recently, the twenty-five-nation SELA (the Latin American Economic System) announced plans to establish its own MNCs. Special priorities will be given agribusiness, low-cost housing, selected capital goods, as well as an inter-American data center. Even the once-hostile Andean Pact, shaken by the recent withdrawal of Chile, is planning its own versions of MNCs and is modifying its earlier pressures on foreign firms to divest and phase out of the continent.

- *Even, East-West multinationals.* Over the past decade, more than 800 joint manufacturing ventures have taken place between Western firms and Eastern European countries. Russia alone has purchased more than 1,000 turnkey plants complete with trained technical staffs. Noted economist, Paul W. McCracken, predicts more to come: "Down the road there may even be growing opportunities for 'joint ventures' to develop the resources of the USSR's Great East, a vast, sparsely populated land reminiscent of our Great West. Russian capital and management must be supplemented if these resources are to be developed vigorously, and this is increasingly recognized there."

Where the strategy is to capture a regional market, we call these coalitions Regional Industrial System Constellations (RISCs). Where the government supports joint ventures with foreign companies to serve the local market, they are called National Industrial System Constellations (NISCs). The French Postal and Telegraph System (PTT) is an example of the latter; Fig. 5.2 shows the set of coalitions supported by the French government in its development of the supplier system for the PTT. Note the involvement of leading companies representing various nations, thus reducing the national influence of a single corporate participant.

1. CIT–Alcatel agreement with Nippon Electric to offer the Japanese D10 exchanges.

2. CIT–Alcatel's subsidiary SLE to offer the AXE switch developed by Swedish L. M. Ericcson.

3. Thomson–CSF with Northern Electric (now Northern Telecom, Canada) to offer the SP-1 exchange.

4. SAT with Germany's Siemens to offer the EWS exchange being installed in West Germany.

5. TRT with Dutch Philips to offer the PRX exchange.

Fig. 5.2 National coalition formed in response to the French Post, Telephone, and Telegraph (PTT).

These cases point to still more corporate constellations—unrestricted by national location, economic standing, or ideology. The challenge of managing these coalitions is staggering, given the complexity of the stakeholder network that often involves at least two foreign governments. As a result, interorganizational relations must be carefully worked through in order to gain the advantages of such a union.

Our study of these coalitions has detected an overriding atmosphere of mutual suspicion and mistrust. This is especially true when one of the participants is dominant in size and potentially has the ability to acquire its partner(s). Some of the most frequently expressed *danger signs* in the functioning of these coalitions include:

- "X nationality has taken over the GISC. We are losing our identity."

- "They are too big to treat us as equals. We are the stepchildren of the GISC."

- "We appear to have agreed that the best way to 'work' together is not to work together."

- "X firm is holding back vital information from the GISC."

- "They compete with us in more countries than they cooperate."

- "We are required to negotiate in their language and hence we frequently lose arguments."

- "Decision making is too slow and bureaucratic."

- "They have not assigned their best people to the GISC."

- "Our GISC doesn't have the right companies in it; we are missing some important ones."

- "Other GISCs have multigovernment support."

- "Antitrust will dissolve or greatly limit our GISC."

- "There is increasing unwillingness to establish regional or global multicultural structures of a durable type."

- "There's a general belief that synergy is zero or negative."

- "Mediocre decision making is accepted, because it takes too long to get a really good decision."

- "People who have little influence are assigned to joint projects."

- "There is a belief that synergy just happens."

To date, few OD efforts have been made to resolve these difficulties.[5] But our experience shows the following characteristics to be found in the more successful coalitions:

- persuasion and participation rather than command;

- a unified and qualified top team with credibility in the mother organizations;

- objectives and capabilities of each component system are known to the other component systems;

- reward system connected to objective attainment;

- early problem detection system for win-lose relationships;

- interface personnel skilled at breaking through communication blocks;

- periodic audits on the perceived reciprocity in the alliance;

- common culture building through management seminars.

To be sure, new insights will be needed on the functioning of multiunit organizations with no locus of central authority. In part, managerial learning from other organizational settings will be transferable. For the most part, however, fundamental changes in our understanding of these complex multiorganizations will be required.

FURTHER IMPLICATIONS

The emergence of these corporate coalitions also demonstrates a waning corporate allegiance to the flag of the parent country. For with multiple alliances, it becomes almost impossible to determine the "parent" country and to assess the true identity of the firm.

Even for more traditional MNCs, the location of their corporate headquarters is often viewed as a serious stumbling block to multinationalism. Take, for example, IBM, which dissolved its World Trade headquarters in New York and replaced it with two international headquarters—IBM Europe (in Paris) and IBM Americas/Far East (in

New York). Can other MNCs with extensive overseas interests expect to enjoy continued success *without* dual or multiple headquarters? Probably not. This does not mean that Volvo, Solvay, and San Miguel will abandon their homes in Sweden, Belgium, and the Philippines. Rather, it suggests that world-class companies, especially those with limited domestic markets, must establish some form of "shadow government" in at least one foreign city.

Far more radical measures, in fact, were recently proposed by the chief executive officers of two leading North American multinationals:

• With the restricted provisions of the proposed Foreign Trade and Investment Act (or Hartke-Burke Bill) receiving considerable support by the United States Congress, relocation of Dow Chemical Company's head office was openly advocated by management. Its former Chairman, Carl Gerstacker, went on record as seriously considering a shift of the company's corporate base "to some remote Caribbean island."

• Only 7 percent of the total sales of Massey-Ferguson Ltd. are generated in its home country, Canada. In 1975, over $2.5 billion in sales revenues were made outside North America. Thus, it surprised very few when Massey-Ferguson's President, Albert A. Thornbrough, said that he meant it when Massey publicly announced that it might move its headquarters from Toronto to Holland. Thornbrough commented, "Oh yes, we would have done it. At most we would have had to move twenty to thirty individuals. The fact that we sit in Toronto doesn't mean a thing. We could function as well in London or Fort Lauderdale."

While seriously considered, both propositions were eventually shelved. Nevertheless, greater mobility of company headquarters is quite likely. In the United States alone, over 15 percent of the MNCs have shifted sites in the last five years. Needless to say, changes of this magnitude in worldwide companies begin to highlight the increasing need for internationally oriented process consultants.

Still, for most firms, the changes are probably considered somewhat extreme and not within reach in this decade. As a result, the regional-headquarters option provides a more direct and less radical structural change that can significantly alter the level of multinationalism in a company. Complementary alternatives to multiple headquarters are:

- building regional centers of competence in, say, R & D, engineering, and marketing, as IBM and SKF have done;

- moving the headquarters of a product division to another country, as Atlas Copco A B and USM Corporation have done;

- establishing regional training modules with worldwide enrollments which focus on key problems like foreign-exchange management or manufacturing problems in developing countries—an approach used by Citibank and Philips;

- developing regional advisory boards, as Westinghouse, Exxon, and Chase Manhattan Bank have done.

Considered together, these trends begin to reveal the shape of multinational corporations of the future—as well as other social institutions that elect to serve them.

SUMMARY

Regionalism is not without its limitations. Most areas of the world are far less homogeneous than regiocentrism assumes them to be. And the degree of homogeneity is subject to widely varying interpretations. It is far easier, for example, for an American to see the "Europeanness" of a German than for a Frenchman to identify this same characteristic in an Englishman. To the American, the Frenchman is blind for not seeing the similarities. To the Frenchman, the American is blind for not seeing the differences. This lack of shared perspective and cultural uniformity has seriously inhibited the growth of regiocentrism.

Despite the problems, regionalism is here to stay. And effective regional organizational forms and management processes are critical to the success of worldwide institutions—especially newly emerging corporate coalitions. With proper care, regional organization development can be an important asset in expanding the global perspective and worldwide effectiveness of the firm.

NOTES

1. Several thoughts contained in this segment were developed in David A. Heenan and Calvin Reynolds, "RPO's: A Step toward Global Human Resources Management." *California Management Review,* Fall 1975. Used with permission.

2. See Gilbert H. Clee and Alfred diScipio, "Creating a World Enterprise," *Harvard Business Review*, November–December 1959; and Clee and Wilbur M. Sachtjen, "Organizing a Worldwide Business," *Harvard Business Review,* November–December 1964.

3. Heenan and Reynolds, op. cit., p. 6.

4. Howard V. Perlmutter, "The Multinational Firm and the Future." *The Annals of the American Academy of Political and Social Science*, September 1972, pp. 139–152.

5. Howard V. Perlmutter, "Notes on the Management of NISCs, RISCs, and GISCs," Working Paper, Wharton School, University of Pennsylvania, 1974.

PART 2
BUILDING A MULTINATIONAL INFRASTRUCTURE

6
BUILDING GLOBAL CITIES

Rising in the shimmering Arizona desert, midway between Phoenix and Flagstaff, is Arcosanti. The brainchild of the noted Italian architect, Paolo Soleri, it is, in the words of its creator, an arcology—a futuristic city combining both architecture and ecology. Scheduled for completion by 1990, Arcosanti will house 3,000 citizens under one roof in an integrated work-and-play environment. As a prototype of bigger things to come, for Soleri it foretells the ultimate design of tomorrow's cities.[1]

As futuristic as Arcosanti may be, its true contribution might be overshadowed by an alternative urban system, the global city.[2] While preserving Soleri's belief that architectural and ecological considerations are paramount, the global-city concept goes one step further by recognizing the economic realities of today and tomorrow. For public executives in several locations, the future development and even survival of their cities depends in large part on their globalization. Indeed, urban planners in a few municipalities (most notably Paris and Coral Gables) have led, not hindered, the multinationalization process. That is why the city of tomorrow will be the global city of today—the city that has set its course on attracting multinational corporate tenants.

But to date, the principal efforts of internationally oriented cities are regiocentric on our EPRG scale, shown in Table 6.1.

Table 6.1

Four Types of Governmental Orientation toward Creating
and Supporting Urban Infrastructures and Utilizing Urban Space

Ethnocentric *(National City)*	*Polycentric* *(Multienclave)*
a) Emphasizes goods and services to be provided for home-country nationals.	a) While reserving a majority of space and supporting institutions of and for home-country na- tionals, permits and encourages
b) Permits only home-country nationals in key positions in urban infrastructures,	b) A variety of infrastructures which support foreign/relatively mono- cultural groups, and institutions, who live in similar space accord- ing to their own standards,
c) And only home-country nationals are given choice space.	c) And separate from the urban space and institutions of home- country nationals,
d) Supports activities, policies, pro- grams which emphasize home- country values, standards, customs.	d) And permitting a great variety of access to choice space and, according to means, may live far better than in home country.
e) Accepts only foreign nationals who are willing to accept home- country objectives, and identify with home-country values, cus- toms, culture while being in an inferior status.	

Regiocentric *(Regional City)*	*Geocentric* *(Global City)*
a) While reserving (often by default) a majority of space and infra- structure to home-country na- tionals, permits and encourages	a) While reserving (often by default) a proportion of space and infra- structures to home-country na- tionals, permits and encourages
b) A variety of multicultural infra- structures with persons and insti- tutions oriented to a given region (e.g., Europe), who evolve regional patterns, standards, and customs which	b) A variety of world-oriented infrastructures of which the following geographical areas are represented: (i) N. America, S. America, E. and W. Europe, Africa, and Asia,
c) Embody the home-country val- ues, standards, and culture as one set of inputs and influences, but whose character is identified as regional,	(ii) advanced and developing countries, and (iii) socialist and capitalistic economic systems.

Table 6.1 *cont'd.*

d) And where no regional groups are "second-class citizens," but where nonregional citizens enjoy lesser privileges.

c) Where no national groups are second-class citizens and enjoy lesser rights and space and privileges than any other nationals,

d) And where customs, values, standards are oriented to universality.

We note that:

1. The *ethnocentric city* has relatively few *international functions* of a durable character, but could support temporary systems, events, and infrastructures, including tourism, conferences, trade fairs, etc. It is monolingual.

2. The *polycentric or multienclave city* will tend to develop a variety of durable infrastructures (schools, hospitals, cultural facilities) to support each national or cultural group. Its international functions will tend to be monocultural. It is multi-monolingual.

3. *The regiocentric or regional city* will tend to develop a variety of multicultural regional structures, mainly to facilitate intercultural accommodation (economic, social, cultural, and educational). Such a city needs to design and develop integrational regional functions of an institutional, transactional, expressive symbolic character. It is multilingual.

4. *The geocentric or global city* will tend to develop a variety of world-oriented infrastructures, including interregional (cultural, educational, social, economic). It has many international functions. It is multilingual and universal-language oriented.

Source: Howard V. Perlmutter, "Scenario A: Paris as a Center for Multinational Enterprise," in *Paris: Ville Internationale*, LA. Documentation Francaise, Vol. 39, 1975, pp. 98-107.

Their focus is on wooing the *regional* offices of North American, European, and Japanese multinational corporations and, to a lesser extent, institutions like trade groups and service bureaus. Prestigious corporate headquarters of worldwide companies are, of course, welcomed. But, for the most part, headquarters have not moved. While, as was mentioned in Chapter 5, important forces of change may alter all this, the thrust of global cities over the next decade will be in the direction of regionalism. What's more, the race is on!

Competition among cities for regional offices today is intense. With much the same zeal shown by national state governments in their efforts to attract foreign direct investment, several cities vie for dominance:

• The European strongholds of London and Brussels are being actively contested by Paris. In 1975, in fact, Paris displaced Brussels in having the largest number of European regional offices of United States companies (seventy-nine to sixty-six).

• In Asia, similarly, Tokyo, Hong Kong, and Singapore are feeling the pressure of Manila and, to a lesser extent, of Honolulu. For example, in relatively short order (since a special 1973 decree by Philippines' President Ferdinand Marcos to accommodate Far Eastern regional offices), Manila has reportedly attracted ninety companies, including GTE International, Rockwell International, Caterpillar Tractor, and North American Van Lines.

• Already dominant as the hub of Latin American business activity, Coral Gables is not content to rest on its laurels. Right now, an aggressive marketing plan, aimed at luring the Latin American regional offices of European multinationals, is being launched.

• All too familiar is the exodus of corporate headquarters from New York, which has suffered a 40 percent loss since 1968. Withdrawal of North American headquarters to the low-density suburbs or sun-belt centers such as Atlanta, Dallas, and Houston is of utmost concern not only to New York, but also to those cities facing similar problems in the northeastern and midwestern United States.

What emerges is a new social institution, with characteristics unlike those of earlier urban systems or the futuristic possibilities of an Arcosanti. For the most part, global cities are evolving in response to some of the fundamental changes in the world's industrial system mentioned earlier. Especially important has been the trend toward regionalism. The drive by MNCs for more regional offices reflects their increased interest in finding new urban locations. And the cities that perceive this need will be the ones to attract corporate tenants. In fact, the Toronto-based International Association for Metropolitan Research and Development (Intermet) has identified corporate globalization as an objective for its membership—221 metropolitan cities with over one million residents.

A TALE OF FOUR CITIES

To measure its commitment to multinationalism, a city must face up to a fundamental question: Can we afford to be excluded from the world economy? To at least four cities—Paris, Coral Gables, Philadelphia, and Honolulu—the answer is a resounding "no." What follows are brief vignettes from the globalization of all four cities; however, in describing a process-oriented approach to multinational urbanization, Honolulu will serve as our primary example.

Paris

The "City of Light" can no longer be accused of the xenophobia of the Gaullist era. Public concern about such behavior, along with the city's decaying physical appearance, prompted a critical reassessment of Paris's future role in the world economy. Parisians were especially worried about the giant steps that Brussels, London, and Geneva had taken toward being well-established continental centers. But with the help of pioneering research at the Wharton School on building global cities, Paris has undergone a major transformation.

Thanks to the efforts of a Wharton School team led by Professors Hasan Ozbekhan and Perlmutter, Paris's goal is to become *the* favored site for European headquarters and financial institutions, as well as for research and development centers. Table 6.2 illustrates a timetable of Paris's intended evolution as a global city. More specifically, the table underscores the need for programmed social interventions, as well as new institutions, in multinationalizing a major urban center.

Critical, too, has been the Delegation de l'Amenagement des Territoires et de l'Action Régionale (DATAR). Since launching its campaign in late 1974, DATAR has attracted such United States corporations as Bendix, Chase Manhattan Bank, Corning Glass Works, Data General, and Revlon. In fact, Paris now ranks second only to London in number of European regional offices of United States multinationals.

Table 6.2
Proposed Indicative Schedule of Evolution

Current Profile of Parts	1970	1980	1990	2000	Outcomes as Defined by Objectives
• National capital			Capital of EEC		• Denationalization
• "Nationalistic" city		Denationalization			• Multinationalization
• Elitist center		Capital of France moved to other city			• Decongestion
• Conservative center					• Change of economic structure
• Authoritarian admin.		Open-city	New social structures		• Change of cultural outlook
• Non-self governing	Self-government				• Change of social organization and relationships
• Costly to France		Technetronic industrial base	"Informatique" design & production		
• "Suction pump" effect		Population limit and deflection			Arising from:
• Reliance on economic rationality		Change of economic activities mix, and			• Political regiocentricity
• Growth through industrialization alone		Increase in postindustrial services			• Economic geocentricity

Table 6.2 cont'd.

Current Profile of Parts	1970	1980	1990	2000	Outcomes as Defined by Objectives
• Weak in financial functions			Multinational functional services		• Urban rationality
			Development of transnational regions		• Postindustrial evolution
• Deteriorating environment			Development of worldwide financial information management system		• Cultural polycentrism
		Multination-alization			
• Francophone LDC-oriented		Regulate city's center	Environmental research/planning/services		
			University of development		Should create the desired GLOBAL CITY
• Culturally "ethno-centric"		LDC product associations			
• City of diminishing creativity in all functions		World center for nonnational cultural events	University of the world		
		Change city's social structure			

Source: H. Ozbekhan, "Composite Scenario," *Paris: Ville Internationale*, Documentation Francaise, Vol. 39, 1974, pp. 108–122.

In large part, the success of Paris is due to the failure of other cities to service their corporate clientele adequately. The British government's repeated bluffs to change tax legislation for foreign executives and the United Kingdom's severe economic problems have made London less appealing than before. Efforts by Belgium to raise taxes on foreign employees have hurt Brussels. Geneva, too, has experienced a withdrawal of regional offices, primarily because of Swiss restrictions on foreign residents.

But Paris's success is also due to the effective communication of its advantages—its central location, ample office space, efficient transportation network, trained office workers, and, of course, the quality of Parisian living.

Paris's ultimate ambition is to be global. Regional offices, President d'Estaing hopes, will eventually lead to the city becoming a worldwide metropolis of corporate headquarters from both the public and the private sector.

Coral Gables

Once a sleepy bedroom community in southern Florida, Coral Gables has become the "Gateway City to Latin America." Today it houses the Latin American regional offices of fifty-six multinational corporations, including Exxon, Gulf Oil, ITT, Uniroyal, and Dow Chemical, as well as the world headquarters of such diverse businesses as dance studios (Arthur Murray, Inc.), security systems (Wachenhut Corp.), and fast foods (Burger King, Inc.).

The story of Coral Gables began in the early 1960s, when the city fathers became concerned about the serious decline in Coral Gables's major industry, retailing. In an effort to broaden the city's tax base, the Office of Community Development investigated several possible nonpolluting, service-oriented industries.

In their search, the city planners stumbled across Jersey Standard's Latin American headquarters, which had moved from Montreal to "the Gables" in 1951. That one move appeared to offer promising possibilities for other multinationals. Therefore, a group of top business and civic leaders formed a committee to assist the Office of Community Development in marketing Coral Gables to other companies with significant Latin American interests.

The effort was successful. By 1967, Dow Chemical, Gulf Oil, and Coca Cola had joined Exxon. Since then, the most enthusiastic marketers of the city have been the transplanted executives from those companies that have moved there.

Today, Coral Gables is actively seeking the Latin American headquarters of European multinationals. To date, two British-owned companies—Imperial Chemical Industries and Tate & Lyle—oversee their South American operations from the Gables.

Moreover, this innovative city is now playing another variation on the Latin theme by wooing the North American regional offices of Latin-owned multinationals. Admittedly, there are fewer such potential tenants, but two companies with substantial business interests in the United States—an Argentinian meat packer and a Brazilian manufacturer of bricks—already maintain regional offices in Coral Gables.

"We've barely scratched the surface of what we can do," says one urban planner. In the years to come, an increasingly varied group of worldwide institutions are likely to be domiciled in this pleasant subtropical setting.

Philadelphia

The social-architectural perspective applied to the "City of Brotherly Love" revealed to researchers some significant similarities and differences between Philadelphia's approach and, in particular, the Paris approach.[4] The most important similarities were illustrated in the following ways:

1. *Appreciative-diagnostic.* Here, researchers analyzed the major global, national, and subnational trends and value changes among the various stakeholder groups. Also investigated were the international strengths and weaknesses of the cities themselves.

2. *Planning* designed to include the following elements:
   - A reference projection or extrapolation of the cities' futures, with the assumption that no major changes were planned for the present premises and policies of their leadership. For Paris, this *consequence analysis* presented the image of Paris as a second-rate city, with a drastic decline in the quality of Parisian living predicted by the year 2000. For Philadelphia, even in the short term, a similar consequence identified was the likelihood of the continued loss of jobs and tax revenues.

- Building scenarios of alternative futures, where the economic, demographic, cultural, technological assets were determined. Through systematically changing a city's future premises and policies, plausible international roles for the city were devised, and leading areas for development of a global perspective considered.

3. *Interventions* that identify specific options for the future and generate the conditions needed to build a more international city. Four areas of intervention appeared:

- *Institutional.* Here, existing institutions altered or reformulated their missions and strategies to accommodate the international future of the city. The museum, for instance, focused on international exhibitions.

- *Multiorganizational* approaches, where diverse organizations—banks, religious institutions, the university—collaborated to develop the international capabilities of the city.

- *International networks and linkages*—organized to assure that the city's assets in industry, culture, and education were known throughout the world. This involved considering overseas marketing offices.

- *Ecosystems*, where the city's natural resources were strengthened. Waterways, parks, and various physical attributes were improved, with the international-city theme as central.

The differences between the Paris and Philadelphia approaches are summarized in Fig. 6.1. The Paris project, with its year 2000 focus, differentiated the cultural, economic, and political changes in terms of ethno-, poly-, regio-, and geocentricity. On the other hand, the Philadelphia project was relatively short term in its orientation (five years). Hence, a grass-roots approach was initiated to mobilize the citizenry to identify those geocentric aspects of the city that could serve as a starting point for its internationalization.

Starting as a joint venture of the Greater Philadelphia Partnership (a group of leading citizens) and the Wharton School, the Philadelphia project gained the support of the city administration midway through the planning phase. Quite the opposite occurred in Paris, where the French government's planning agency, DATAR, served as the project's primary sponsor.

Parameter	Paris as a global city	International City of Philadelphia project
1. Internationalism	Economic geocentricity; political regiocentricity; cultural polycentrism.	Selected domains of geo-centric development: • economic; foreign investment • cultural-events center • health care • conventions and conferences • world education center; grass-roots internationalism
2. Primary clients	French government planning agency: DATAR	A partnership of leading citizens
3. Concept of city of future	An enclave-geocentric city; a mediating or global crossroads city	An American international city: with selected geocentric competence areas, integrative-geocentrism in orientation
4. Time perspective	The year 2000	Five-year milestones
5. Why project undertaken	Deteriorating quality of life in Paris: wanted Paris to be leading city	Likely economic decline of city: needed positive vision of the future
6. Expected basis for viability	MNCs play leading role; also political and cultural center	Five areas of geocentric development: with international business as foundation stone
7. Expected basis for legitimacy	Government support plus foreign stakeholders, including international institutions	1. Wide participation of internal and external stakeholder groups 2. Foreign stakeholders as co-planners

Fig. 6.1 A comparison of two global cities projects: social-architectural approach. (From Howard V. Perlmutter, *Building the International City of Philadelphia: A Planning Process for Grassroots Internationalism,* Philadelphia, Worldwide Institutions Research Group, The Wharton School, University of Pennsylvania, 1977.)

Paris's future concept was of a leading world city; to a degree, it was based on an elitist or enclave concept of geocentrism. The Philadelphia project, on the other hand, began with the encouragement of diverse citizen groups eager to see their city begin progress toward its desired future state. From the outset, grass-roots internationalism dominated the Philadelphia project. To illustrate, plans were made to connect Philadelphia's international future with the current concerns of its disadvantaged groups (especially black, unemployed teenagers), to identify future job opportunities from international business, and to relate these programs to potential foreign investments.

Honolulu

Despite its attractive mid-Pacific location, the island state of Hawaii is groping for economic choices beyond tourism and agribusiness. Many executives find the conception of its capital city, Honolulu, as "the Coral Gables or the Paris of the Pacific" to be appealing and realistic. No doubt, Honolulu has its share of disadvantages: long distances to the markets of major countries (and the related problems of jet lag and restricted telecommunications), high prices, and limited public education.

To its proponents, however, Honolulu's geographical setting and its ties to Asia make it an interesting contender as the regional hub of the Pacific. Consider its major competition:

Tokyo is virtually pricing itself out of the market. Apartment rentals of $2,000 to $3,000 a month are typical to sustain even a junior executive. Also, acute pollution and urban decay now make the city one of the least preferred living spots in Asia.

Hong Kong suffers from much the same problems. Its cost of living is almost on a par with Tokyo's, and the "Manhattanization" of the tiny island colony bothers many expatriates, particularly those seeking fresh air and open space for their families.

Manila has been making an active bid for regional dominance, but the nation's martial law and visits by Philippines' President and Mrs. Marcos to Cuba, Hanoi, and the Republic of China tend to send chills up the spines of corporate executives based in communities like Peoria, Illinois and Southfield, Michigan, where headquarters decisions are made.

Singapore, under Prime Minister Lee Kuan Yew's leadership, has much in its favor. As the Asian dollar hub and the world's third-largest refining center, it has provided a favorable base for foreign investors. Still, certain recent developments—the United

States military services withdrawal from Southeast Asia, the death of neighboring Malaysia's Prime Minister, and the recent coup in Thailand—call into question Singapore's political stability.

So, the diminishing strength of its competitive cities in Asia, coupled with an intense felt need for economic diversification, may make the timing right for Honolulu to consider regionalism.

To a degree, the city enjoys a modest track record. Through historical accident, a number of leading multinationals already have corporate headquarters in Honolulu, where, of course, these firms began: C. Brewer, Castle & Cooke, Dillingham, Alexander & Baldwin, Amfac, and others.

In addition, twenty-three corporations, including ITT-Sheraton Hotels, United Airlines, Continental Airlines, Northrop Corporation, and Hughes Aircraft Company, maintain regional offices in Honolulu. Add to these such nonprofit institutions as the East-West Center, the Pacific Forum, and the Japan-America Institute of Management Science, also domiciled on the islands, and it becomes apparent that Honolulu may have the core ingredients for globalism.

But how to make this dream a reality? Over two years ago, a MOD program designed to make Honolulu a global city was undertaken by the University of Hawaii's Business School, with the assistance of the state's Department of Economic Planning and Development and the local Chamber of Commerce. The ultimate objectives were ambitious: to attract thirty-four Asia-Pacific regional units by 1980, and forty-eight by 1985. In the entry phase, however, the premium was on diagnosis. More specifically, those of us involved in the project attempted to answer such thorny questions as:

- What are the principal advantages of going global? What benefits can a community expect to enjoy?

- What key factors influence a multinational company in making its headquarters decision?

- How is Honolulu viewed by MNCs in comparison to other competitive cities?

- How could and should community involvement be stimulated in Honolulu's multinationalization?

To answer these questions, extensive interviews were held with senior executives in more than thirty multinational corporations and a mailed questionnaire was completed by executives in sixty multinational companies. In addition, a major planning and commitment-building session, attended by key members of the private and public sector, was held. Vital participants in these meetings were representatives from Coral Gables and the Wharton School's Paris team. Their role was to present demonstration projects of the multinationalization of both cities. Partial results from this research follow.

TANGIBLE AND INTANGIBLE BENEFITS

Of course, each city will have its own reasons for tracking the multinationals. For some cities, economic incentives—more jobs, additional tax revenues, and greater industrial diversification—are the primary spurs. But for others, noneconomic considerations, such as the desire to halt urban decay, cultural erosion, and the diminishing quality of life, are more important. In our search, we found some of the most obvious benefits of globalization to include:

• *Tax revenues.*   Depending on its size and composition, the taxable wage bill of a city's headquarters employees may run from several million to several hundred million dollars. In the case of Coral Gables, the estimates exceed $30 million. Less important, but not insignificant, are property taxes. Of least consequence is the potential from corporate income taxes, since the profits of the typical corporation are earned by its operational companies with relatively little income allocated to headquarters. When all sources are considered, however, global cities realize a sizable net gain in tax revenues from the multinational corporations.

• *Expenditure effects.*   It goes without saying that the aftertax income of MNCs and their employees will be spent in large part on local goods and services. But other expenditures in the local economy are often overlooked. For example, consider the purchases by visitors to headquarters cities. On their way through regional offices or corporate headquarters for budget presentations, management seminars, or home leave, companies' foreign-service contingents wield considerable purchasing power. Their demand alone for the latest appliances, fashions, and gourmet cuisine represents over $10 million to one major Asian city.

So, whether it means reducing unused office space or lining the pockets of local restauranteurs, the primary and secondary effects of headquarters spending are quite considerable.

- *Employment opportunities.* Head offices are not labor-intensive. The average size of staffs in regional and corporate headquarters number 30 and 120, respectively. Besides, local hiring is usually confined to unskilled and clerical employees, with top managerial slots reserved for incumbents.

Usually, however, there are some spillover effects. Accounting firms, banks, advertising agencies, and the like, which sell supporting services to the multinational corporations, should have expanded job opportunities. Thus, while attracting the headquarters of companies would not be the answer to Honolulu's unemployment problems, some employment gains may be expected from it.

The advantages of increased tax revenues, local expenditures, and employment, though substantial, are frequently overshadowed by an intangible benefit: call it "prestige." What better way to diversify a city's economic base than through these nonpolluting, knowledge-oriented command posts? "Blue chips? No, they're gold chips!" a former mayor of Coral Gables remarked.

Community enrichment occurs on many fronts. Often accompanying the arrival of multinational corporate tenants is an overall upgrading of the business community. Professionalism tends to rise; bank tellers learn courtesy and efficiency; even public officials become more responsive.

Behind the scenes, however, a more fundamental change shapes the future image of the city. A multinational corporation brings with it a group of executives who are prime movers in their adopted community. Their strategic positions in international business afford the community a unique overview of the social, political, and economic conditions of the international or regional network.

This knowledge base, once established, is difficult for other cities to match. For Honolulu, this meant telling the world, "We know Asia. It is impossible to conduct business in this part of the world without headquartering here." This perceived monopoly of regional expertise on Asia and the Pacific Basin, the project team felt, could ensure the economic well-being of our community.

A MATTER OF CHOICE

With so much to be gained for Honolulu, it was essential to identify the critical trade-offs chief executives make in their choice of possible regional office sites: Do multinationals prefer to locate their regional units closer to major countries' markets or to corporate headquarters? Are tax incentives more important than easy access to air transportation, efficient telecommunications, or high-quality schooling? Does the political stability of a regional site offset all other considerations?

By using conjoint analysis, the project team was able to determine the trade-offs and their relative importance to corporate executives when evaluating global cities.[4] Through our research on the multinationals, sixteen factors were identified that influence the regional-office-location decision. These range from proximity to corporate or international headquarters to supporting infrastructure and services. After constructing various combinations of the sixteen options, we asked executives to rank the combinations from "most preferred" to "least preferred." Their answers, when translated into utility scores from "low" (0) to "high" (5), reflect the relative importance of each factor, as shown in Fig. 6.2.

As the figure shows, most important to international executives are a city's political stability, its supporting infrastructure, the cost of maintaining an expatriate staff, air transportation, and communications. Of least concern are proximity to corporate or international headquarters, tax and related incentives, housing, educational and medical facilities, and availability of office space and personnel. With few exceptions, these results hold for cities in all key regional markets—that is, regardless of the continent under consideration, virtually identical factors prevail in determining the final choice of a city.

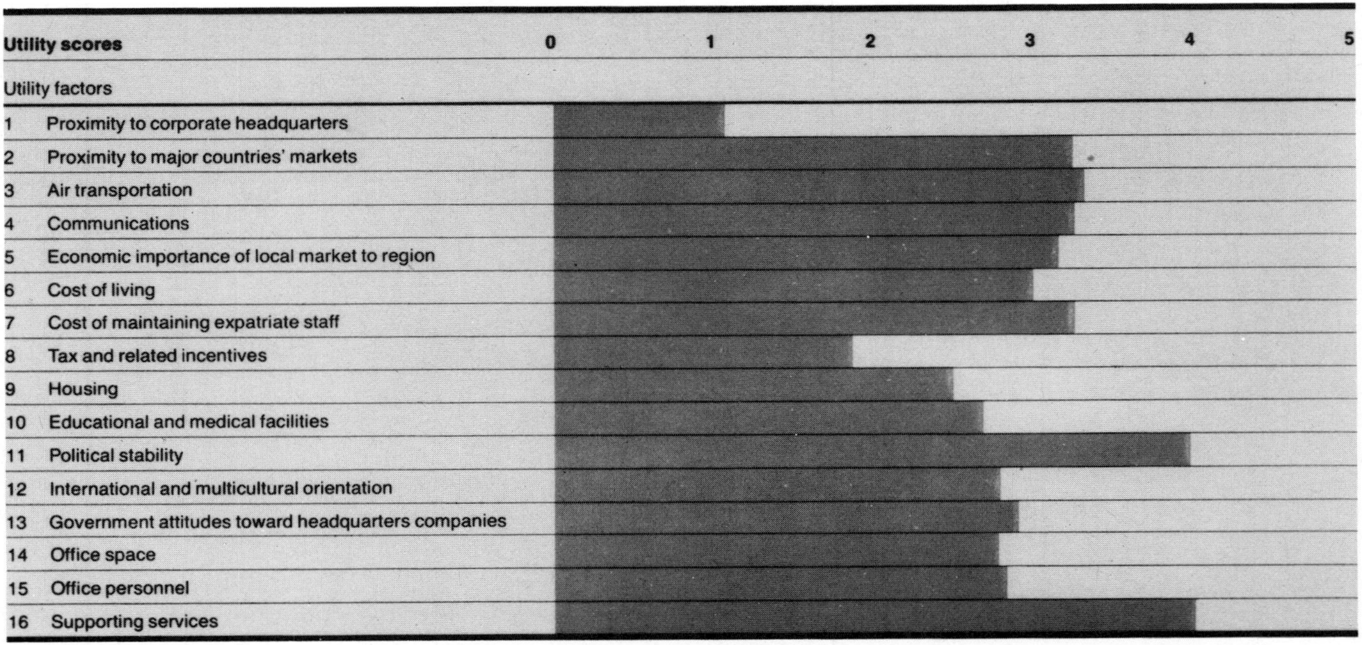

Fig. 6.2 Factors affecting the choice of regional office cities. (From David A. Heenan, "Global Cities of Tomorrow," *Harvard Business Review*, May–June 1977, p. 85. Copyright © 1977 by the President and Fellows of Harvard College.)

INTERESTING ISSUES

Perhaps more important, the information in Fig. 6.2 provided urban planners in Hawaii with intriguing insights into the value systems of chief executives. In particular, these findings helped resolve five areas of concern affecting the choice of regional-office cities such as Honolulu.

Myth of Price

The market for the headquarters business is oligopolistic. The barriers to entry are high, and relatively few cities in any one geographic area are truly competitive. Thus performance, not price competition, prevails.

Our analysis of headquarters cities shows that the importance of economic factors is often greatly overestimated. Herbert E. Meyer, associate editor of *Fortune,* concurs: "Economic considerations are not decisive . . . when it comes to moving a company's headquarters. For most companies that have worldwide operations, the savings are too small to have a discernible effect on earnings."[5] Indeed, many of the companies fleeing from New York City for the Connecticut suburbs fully anticipated *higher* incremental costs for lease rentals, office staff, the professional support services, plus the costs of a physical relocation.

So, too, with location incentives—tax breaks, cash grants, industrial-revenue bonds, and other gimmicks. While some economists argue against disrupting the free-market mechanism with such artificial incentives, more powerful arguments have been established by empirical research. Several studies clearly indicate that location incentives have, at best, only a slight influence over plant-location decisions.[6]

Incentives have even less influence over a move of headquarters. Contrary to popular opinion, the location of its headquarters does not substantially affect the total amount of taxes a company pays.[7] This fact correlates with our finding that chief executives think tax and related incentives are of low utility.

Nor are city fathers eager to compete on the basis of price. As Ken Smith, director of community development for Coral Gables, remarked in our planning session, "A city relying on tax and other giveaways can always be underpriced. The headquarters business is volatile enough without introducing cutthroat competition." Needless to say, Honolulu was not prepared to offer special tax breaks to MNCs.

Even without special incentives, however, if a city is to be competitive, its general economic climate must be positive. If its cost of doing business far exceeds its competitors', it will lose out. Consider the recent rush of United States and European multinationals to Makati, situated on the outskirts of Manila. Makati's gain comes at the expense of Tokyo and Hong Kong—two cities that many Asia watchers feel have priced themselves out of the market.

On a similar score, Paris's increase in European headquarters activity has been caused, in part, by an overheated Belgian economy. The 30–40 percent cost-of-living differential that Brussels once enjoyed over Paris has narrowed—to the advantage of the French captial.

Costs to maintain expatriates, however, are somewhat different, and, in many locations, there are significant cost disadvantages for multinationals that maintain expatriates in foreign-based regional offices. Approximately 50–80 percent of the executives staffing these units receive some form of overseas allowance aimed at "keeping a person whole"—that is, providing overseas executives with the same net income they would have earned had they remained at home. These intensive foreign-service payments are eliminated, of course, when the company relocates its regional units within the parent company.

Predictably, this will mean the increasing reliance of American multinationals on foreign nationals (always a wise move), as well as a "Yankee, come home" movement among MNCs. Given the rising importance of expatriate costs, we can look for possible windfall gains for American-based global cities such as Honolulu.

Meaning of Proximity

Which is more important—to be closer to major countries' markets or to be closer to corporate headquarters? As Fig. 6.2 indicates, most worldwide companies prefer to locate their regional headquarters in cities relatively close to their major operational units. Faster communications, reduced jet lag, and better market information are some of the reasons mentioned. True, some businesspersons stress the need for close ties to corporate headquarters in the parent country. No matter how decentralized a company's organizational philosophy, a regional unit cannot afford to cut itself off from corporate headquarters. On balance, however, proximity to the markets of key countries is of most importance.

To a degree, of course, proximity—to other countries' markets at least—may be a state of mind. Despite the lengthy flying time from Coral Gables to several Latin markets (up to eight hours in the case of Argentina and the west coast of South America), the city has been able to compensate for this apparent limitation. Not so for Honolulu, where the time-zone changes are much more demanding. Thus, if Honolulu is to succeed in its globalization, its appeal must be made on somewhat different locational considerations.

Useful in this regard may be the concept of an urban crossroads, a city linking regional blocs with the corporate superpowers. In more peaceful times, Beirut played this role, bridging the gap between the Arab world and the important European commercial centers of Paris, London, and Zurich. By the same token, French planners dream of Paris being a "privileged crossroads" where diverse institutions might conduct their affairs. Worldwide collective bargaining, commodities arbitrage, and commercial negotiations between developed and developing countries could all take place in this neutral site.

To some international executives, an urban crossroads provides the best vantage point for understanding the political economics of nearby regions. A broad perspective of, say, Latin America and of how the North American multinational corporation relates to it is difficult to acquire in Caracas, São Paulo, or any other city buried within the South American continent. While a location within the region provides immediate access to countries within the area, it may obstruct a full understanding of the realities of the Latin American viewpoint. The most successful global settings in the next decade may be those that can provide a broad perspective of the key cities in the world economy. And, quite often, as with Coral Gables and Honolulu, these crossroads cities will be at the boundaries of major market areas.

One executive, based in Coral Gables, insists, "Here, in three hours, I can find out more about the happenings in Latin America than I could there in three weeks in any of its locations." Similarly, the recent record of companies that have left New York for supposedly isolated locations indicates that they are not out of the corporate mainstream. To the contrary, there has been little or no fall-off in vital information or supporting services.

There are other benefits of locating in a crossroads city. For one, it lessens the likelihood of the corporate headquarters being identified with any one country. The early advantages of Brussels as a European commercial center were based on its low profile. Its mayor, Pierre Van Alteren, suggests that "since we're small and have no nuclear ambitions, we can't be accused of being imperialists."[8] No one thinks of a Brussels-headquartered company as being "too Belgian." But for multinationals with headquarters in London or Paris, the charges of being "too British" or "too French" are more serious.

The need for organizational neutrality is even more acute in those areas dominated by one especially powerful nation, such as Japan or Brazil. For several leading MNCs—Pfizer, Dow Chemical, and others—it has been necessary to move their regional offices from São Paulo and Tokyo to more neutral sites, often at the perimeter of the region. Such a shift demonstrates to nationals of other countries in the region that the corporation is truly multinational, not the favorite son of the dominant country. Such a move also minimizes the risk of a regional unit becoming immersed in the operational problems of the host country, and most multinationals follow a "hands-off" approach for their local operations while they retain control of strategic issues at the corporate headquarters level.

Nevertheless, certain circumstances may make it appropriate to locate the regional office closer to its operational affiliates—for example, a major start-up, a change of ownership, unprofitable operations, or government difficulties in several countries in the region. Conversely, other conditions, ranging from the high cost of maintaining a separate area headquarters to the political ambitions of the regional vice president for additional corporate visibility, may make integrating the regional office with corporate headquarters feasible. In the final analysis, the answer to the question of location depends on a multitude of such variables, all subject to frequent change.

No one is more aware of the volatility of corporate headquarters decisions about location than urban planners. Their vocabulary builds on terms such as "net additions" (the number of new head-quarters gained less the inevitable departures); their planning horizon is abbreviated (two to four years is the usual gestation period for MNCs to reach a decision about headquarters); and their effective market share may represent only 5 percent of the number of serious corporate inquiries.

To be sure, competing for one of today's most mobile social institutions, the corporate headquarters, is no place for the faint-hearted. As Bush Hatley, vice president of business development at the Dallas Chamber of Commerce, put it, "There's a lot more work than . . . results in this business."[9] Notwithstanding the disappointments, in Honolulu it was felt that the benefits of building a corporate city far exceed the costs.

Adequacy of Financial Services

We next asked, "Can a city become truly global or even regional in a business sense without also becoming an international financial center?" By "international financial center," we meant a money and capital market location whose participants (especially the financial intermediaries) have significant international relationships. It is an institutional hub that performs a wide range of services, including simple depository facilities, trade financing, and exchange arbitrage.

The most significant international financial centers—London and New York—evolved primarily as strong national financial hubs eager to serve a domestic clientele with international interests. Less comprehensive ones, such as Hong Kong, Singapore, and until recently Beirut, developed as convenience centers for foreign financial institutions attracted to the region.

But, in the view of at least one international banker, Monroe J. Haegele of First Pennsylvania Bank, all such centers should possess an adequate financial infrastructure, a favorable regulatory environment, freedom from confiscatory measures, and a strong historical role in commerce.[10]

This standard is difficult to achieve. Even Paris, with its well-developed national money and capital markets, concedes that its chance of becoming the financial hub of Europe in this decade is most unlikely. London, the center of the Eurocurrency market, Zurich, and Frankfurt will continue to dominate European finance for the foreseeable future. Nevertheless, the recent success of Paris and others indicates that Honolulu could achieve global or regional economic dominance *without* providing integrated international financial services.

Coral Gables is an example. While the Coral Gables–Miami area is attempting to upgrade its level of international financial competence (it now ranks second only to New York in the number of Edge Act banks), executives there are of the opinion that New York will always remain the financial center for Latin America.

As one area executive commented, "Our financial needs in Coral Gables are quite simple, and we should be realistic about them. All we really seek are adequate personal banking facilities for our Latin and expatriate staff and some basic economic intelligence. Beyond that, New York takes charge."

Thus, global cities need not be full-service bankers to attract regional or corporate headquarters. A comprehensive infrastructure, as shown in Fig. 6.2, is a plus; and the more integrated the service network of any urban environment, the greater its likelihood for success.

For Honolulu, the starting point may be simply an environment where visitors from at home and abroad feel comfortable and are at ease in conducting their business affairs. Note that in all three cities discussed, tourists have played a major role in their globalization. Demands by vacationers for first-rate hotel, restaurant, and transportation facilities have meant a better support system for multinational corporation executives as well.

Too much of a good thing, of course, can be detrimental. Both Honolulu and Coral Gables must constantly downplay their undeserved image as tropical paradises where only suntans, not hard business results, are earned. That a city's airlines are accessible, its streets safe, its shopkeepers smiling, and its skies usually sunny should promote, not retard, its headquarters potential. In our opinion, there is a strong complementary relationship between a city's tourist industry and its quest for leadership in international business.[11]

Fortunately, no one location enjoys an absolute advantage over another. Instead, global cities, like global companies, frequently adopt strategies that build on their particular strengths. One sees this fact at work today in cities such as Hartford (insurance), Nice (research and development), and Rotterdam (oil refining). More-over, achieving world expertise in one industrial field may lead to a broader definition of a global city's span of competence. Success in one dimension often brings about success in others.

Emergence of Urban Satellites

Today, three out of every four Americans live in cities—a percent-age slightly less than Germany's (82 percent) and the United King-dom's (80 percent), but somewhat more than that of France (70 percent) or Spain (59 percent). Still, urbanologists are divided over the future directions of the world's cities. Some, such as noted city planner Edmund Bacon, predict an economic resurgence of inner cities and corporate commitment to them. Others, seemingly in the majority, forecast a steady exodus from the traditional cities and observe that, for the first time in American history, cities have been growing at a slower rate than rural areas; these experts even suggest that the United States is destined to become the first industrialized country *without* important cities.[12]

No matter what scenario is selected, a rising anticity sentiment is emerging in corporate boardrooms throughout the world. For chief executive officers today, new suburban names—Fairfield County, Oak Brook, and Makati—are replacing the old familiar ones of New York, Chicago, and Manila. Fairfield County, for instance, now ranks third (behind New York and Chicago) in the number of "*Fortune* 500" companies headquartered there. In the South, Coral Gables represents still another case for the urban satellite.

But why Coral Gables? Why not Miami? "There's only one reason," commented J. William Cochran, senior executive-in-resi-dence for ICI United States Inc. "Coral Gables went after the busi-ness." Ironically, the top officials in its Office of Community Development began their careers in Miami, where many of the ini-tial concepts of building a headquarters city were developed.

But Miami was unable to secure the necessary support for regionalism. Frustrated, its best city planners moved to Coral Gables and won the support of this smaller, more cohesive commu-nity. Subsequently, a nucleus of regional offices was established; Coral Gables has never looked back.

To be sure, the ability of suburbs to develop timely commitments to multinational corporations in an environment relatively free of the problems of urban decay, crime, and depression gives them special advantages over traditional cities. Nonetheless, very few urban satellites can expect to make it as global economic centers. As demonstrated earlier, efficient air transportation and communications links with the rest of the world are crucial for headquarters sites. Without an easy ten-minute drive to the Miami International Airport, Coral Gables would not have achieved its current level of success.

Even when corporations are willing to settle outside the big metropolises, they are not moving too far out. Some kind of center is essential, and companies rarely move off by themselves to the wilderness.[13] Moreover, this vital nucleus of headquarters companies develops only when they can be assured of the first-rate facilities of a traditional urban center. Honolulu, in the minds of many, captures the major benefits of a global city without its costs.

The Importance of Political Stability

As we have seen, political stability is a dominant consideration in selecting a regional-office city. But with the velocity of change in the world economy, the only certainty is future uncertainty. How, with any degree of accuracy, can a chief executive analyze the economic effects of falling dominoes in Southeast Asia, the swelling hostilities in South Africa, or the aftereffects of a new Administration in the United States? Clearly, events of this nature influence the course of conduct of global companies and their cities.

Witness the case of Beirut. Once termed the "Paris of the Middle East," Beirut was considered too important to come under attack. Yet today, despite its attractive and strategic location, Beirut's hopes of expanding its former role as the commercial center of the Middle East are all but shattered by continual outbreaks of violence between Christians and Moslems. More than 40,000 lives have been lost and more than $3 billion in damages has occurred. Nearly all of the multinational companies domiciled in the city have either reduced their staffs or pulled out altogether— with Athens, Amman, Bahrain, and Cairo actively striving to become the refugee center for Beirut-based executives and their families. Needless to say, Beirut's dreams of regional leadership have been postponed indefinitely.

For top executives, the lesson of Beirut is to examine with care the likely fortunes of potential corporate command posts. Similar to Beirut, other supposedly "buffered" cities, such as Hong Kong, Singapore, and Berlin, may be extremely fragile. Severe discontinuity in their internal operations is the risk that must be accepted by multinational corporations located in such cities. And, no doubt, the rise in headquarters activity in low-risk areas like Honolulu is a measure of the increasing political uncertainties around the world.

ANALYZING URBAN COMPETITION

Figure 6.2 identifies senior executives' order of preference for sixteen features of regional office sites. While useful, this information does not pinpoint where companies will eventually locate. Thus, in the Honolulu project, it was critical to see which Asia-Pacific cities compete most effectively with each other and on what terms they do this.

As Table 6.3 shows, it is possible to consolidate the lengthy list of sixteen items into four central categories under which headquarters compete. By asking executives to rank ten cities (including the corporate-headquarters city) according to this reduced list, one can acquire a visual representation of the nature of regional competition. Figure 6.3, the product of a multidimensional mapping program, shows the ranking Asia-Pacific regional-office sites, including Honolulu.

Note that there is no clear winner. The spread of the dimensional arrows indicates that international executives tend to distinguish sharply between various Asian headquarters sites, depending on the dimension in question. While Singapore and Hong Kong are highly regarded for their strategic importance, both cities fall far short of the mark when it comes to quality of life and infrastructure. For these attributes, San Francisco and Honolulu are considered the leaders.

Also note that the corporate-headquarters city has relatively low appeal to top managers as an Asia-Pacific headquarters center. Observe too that while Manila is virtually "out of it" on the map, it has enjoyed the greatest recent upswing in regional offices—an estimated 150 percent gain in 1976. This change suggests that, notwithstanding a city's deficiences, a strong commitment by its officials can still make it truly competitive.

Using this type of multivariate analysis, urban planners in Honolulu were able to identify what their competition is and the dimensions along which it takes place. Corporate decision makers, too, can assess the headquarters cities that elect to serve them.

Most important, the empirical research conducted in the entry phase of this change program provided direction for the subsequent phases. Survey feedback sessions of this data, for example, crystallized the level of commitment needed to make Honolulu a global city. Further, it enabled community leaders to understand the conditions under which such an effort would be fully acceptable.

Table 6.3
Four Central Attributes of Choice Process

Economic considerations

Economic importance of local market to region
Cost of living
Cost of maintaining expatriate staff
Tax and related incentives

Quality of life

Political stability
Housing
Educational and medical facilities
International and multicultural orientation

Infrastructure

Office space
Office personnel
Government attitudes toward headquarters companies
Supporting services

Strategic importance

Proximity to corporate headquarters
Proximity to the markets of other countries
Air transportation
Communications

Source: David A. Heenan, "Global Cities of Tomorrow," *Harvard Business Review*, May-June 1977, p. 91. Copyright © 1977 by the President and Fellows of Harvard College.

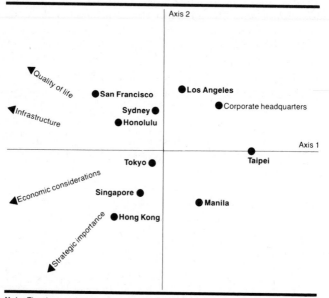

Note: The closer an image is to the head end of the arrows, the more it is credited with possessing the attribute associated with each vector. To compare cities along any one vector, simply mark a position on the arrow by dropping a line perpendicular to the arrow from each headquarters location.

Fig. 6.3 CEOs ratings of ten Asia-Pacific regional-office locations. (From David A. Heenan, "Global Cities of Tomorrow," *Harvard Business Review,* May–June 1977, p. 92. Copyright © 1977 by the President and Fellows of Harvard College.)

BUILDING INDISPENSABLE CITIES

The extent to which any human settlement becomes global in scope depends, in large part, on its citizenry. This globalization occurs only when the permanent residents of the community are convinced that attracting regional offices and corporate headquarters is essential for the city's future survival and growth. Communities that attempt to globalize without co-opting the participation of its permanent citizenry court trouble.

The implications for city planners and corporate executives may be well worth considering. For global cities of the future to flourish, a broad base of community support must be present. The golden ghettos of Forbes Park, Waterloo, and Greenwich, which adjoin Manila, Brussels, and New York respectively, not only reflect corporate inattention to the problems of inner cities but also offer dissidents highly visible targets.

Disaffected segments of any urban society simply will not allow the multinationals, already the subject of intensive scrutiny, to promote such dual economies. For corporate leaders, too, unbalanced growth is bad business, for it detracts from the fundamentally positive effects of private enterprise.

Accordingly, a few farsighted executives are taking the lead to demonstrate the contributions that world corporations can make to urban development. Walter Wriston and Henry Ford II, in particular, have supported the construction of whole new urban environments, in New York and Detroit respectively. Whether rebuilding our traditional inner cities for the global decades ahead is realistic, however, remains unanswered.

Planners should also not forget that cities are *centers of living*. Attention only on the corporate assessment of a city's strengths and weaknesses without consideration of the individuals to be relocated spells disaster.

In the Paris project, the following perceptions were expressed by corporate wives on that city's desirability as a locus for living:

Driving forces	*Restraining forces*
1. Access to expatriate groups of many nationalities.	1. Inefficient environment for living.

Driving forces	*Restraining forces*
2. Possibility of going home for weekends (for British respondents only).	2. Foreigners penalized, especially with respect to taxes.
3. Paris-West: beautiful village setting.	3. Serious psychic problems in the American community.
4. Paris more interesting city than Brussels.	4. Adjustment difficulties, including an unpleasant bureaucracy.
5. Those who know French and understand the culture are well received.	5. Nice place to visit, but not to live in.
6. Availability of the American Hospital.	6. Hard to make French friends or be accepted in French society.
7. Safety in the streets.	7. Limited availability of international and national schools.

Thus, if a city elects to go global, separate planning processes must be established to solicit the views of transplanted expatriate families.

One point is clear: If the constructive impact of globalization is to be realized, collaborative approaches between diverse citizen groups are needed. Hence, the commitment to build a global city requires full community endorsement—from the private and public sectors, labor unions, even religious and educational institutions.

Without such broad-based support, world corporations run the risk of surly customs officials, exploitative realtors, and chauvinistic communities. To find a niche in society for global cities, corporate executives and urban planners must depend on their shared appreciation of the conditions that make global cities indispensable.

Indeed, *indispensability* has been at the heart of urban multinationalization. Whether the cities described above can make it as global cities will only be answered by time. Presently, however, there is well-deserved optimism. But without a program of careful diagnosis and scheduled interventions, such bold undertakings never would have been initiated. In the years to come, MOD will play a major role in building the global cities of the future.

SUMMARY

Today, in several corners of the world, process consultants are working to develop model corporate cities with global aims. Special attention has been focused on four: Paris, Coral Gables, Philadelphia, and Honolulu. While each city is unique, with its own motivations for multinationalization, general implications can be drawn from the experiences of these cities for chief executives and urban planners alike.

Not every city, of course, can be global. But to survive the decades ahead, communities must develop some capability, defined in their own terms, to serve a multinational constituency. In an increasingly interdependent world, our greatest challenge, Buckminster Fuller warns, is not how we get on independently, but how we get on together. Ensuring such international collaboration is the essence of the social-architectural approach to multinational OD. Through its application, peaceful coexistence in the years ahead may be realized in world-oriented cities.

NOTES

1. Paolo Soleri, *Arcology: The City in the Image of Man* (Cambridge, Mass.: MIT Press, 1971).

2. David A. Heenan, "Global Cities of Tomorrow," *Harvard Business Review*, May–June 1977, pp. 79–92.

3. Howard V. Perlmutter, *Building the International City of Philadelphia: A Planning Process for Grassroots Internationalism* (Philadelphia: Worldwide Institutions Research Group, The Wharton School, University of Pennsylvania, 1977).

4. For a discussion of conjoint analysis and other related techniques, see David A. Heenan and Robert A. Addleman, "Quantitative Techniques for Today's Decision Makers," *Harvard Business Review*, May–June 1976, p. 32.

5. Herbert E. Meyer, "Why Corporations Are on the Move," *Fortune*, May 1976, p. 253.

6. See "A Counterattack in the War Between the States," *Business Week*, June 21, 1976, p. 71.

7. Meyer, "Why Corporations are on the Move," p. 253.

8. Daniel Yergin, "Brussels," *The Atlantic*, June 1976, p. 16.

9. See Craig Endicott, "Corporate Relocation: A Rose or a Barb," *The Dallas Times Herald*, 7 December 1975, p. 1-K.

10. Monroe J. Haegele, "Iran's Potential as a Financial Center," *International Finance*, February 23, 1976, p. 7.

11. This relationship was first observed by Harry G. Johnson in "Panama as a Regional Financial Center," *Economic Development and Cultural Change*, January 1976, p. 266.

12. See Jack Patterson, "The Prospect of a Nation with No Important Cities," *Business Week*, February 2, 1976, p. 66.

13. Ibid.

7
INTEGRATED AREA DEVELOPMENT

The role of private direct investment in the developing countries remains widely debated. On the one hand, its proponents contend that only private investment from foreign and domestic sources can alleviate the despair of impoverished nations. Capital-starved economies, they argue, need the investment opportunities that private enterprise alone can contribute. With such capital, new jobs are provided along with much-needed transfers of technology, research and development, and managerial training. In addition, private corporations can best meet the rising expectations of consumers in the Third and Fourth Worlds. In short, there is no end to the tangible and intangible benefits that can accrue to those developing nations eager to attract private investment; and the nations most often cited as showcases are Mexico, Singapore, South Korea, and the Republic of China.

On the other hand, the critics of private enterprise in economic development seem to be gaining increasing sympathy in national and international circles.[1] In their vehement attack on multinational corporations, some authors have reintroduced the enclave case against private investment in developing countries.[2] Shared by many, the enclave rationale is that, far too often, the product of big business is a highly developed area—a petroleum refinery, tourist complex, or international banking center—which coexists with a shantytown environment in which the majority of the population lives at the subsistence level. Inadequate linkages between these dual economies, the critics argue, are major concerns.

Excluded from the alleged gains of investment capital, the argument continues, the local populace can look forward only to continued impoverishment and, even worse, cultural inferiority. "At a deeper level," Robert Wenkam contends, "This attitude of civilized man toward simpler societies and lifestyles implies a basic disrespect of people and the failure to respect fellow man's creations as equal both in spirituality and endowed potentialities."[3]

No doubt, this view is compounded by the profile of global business in the developing world. Well over one-half of all foreign investment in emerging nations is in agribusiness, extractive, and related processing investment. Needless to say, these very industries are frequently the first targets of a government expropriation or takeover. And the sensitivity that any nation attaches to its natural resources is quite understandable. In fact, world public opinion on this matter is most explicit.

In its "doctrine of economic self-determination," the United Nations (and other international legal tribunals) recognize that "Peoples may, *for their own ends*, freely dispose of their national wealth and resources without prejudice to any obligations arising out of . . . international economic agreements." Self-interest, of course, can be expressed only by the nation in question, and MNCs operating in less-developed countries must observe this internationally acknowledged standard.

In the boardrooms of enlightened companies, this creates little difficulty. CEOs in such enterprises are careful to identify the need to modify their viability objectives. That is, to survive overseas, firms are fully prepared to rationalize their profits. In these cases, well-intentioned MNCs:

- Undertake full-scale manufacturing in overseas countries with limited market potential. Although the scope of such operations may be economically infeasible, companies are sympathetic to national needs to expand production.

- Integrate local nationals in the hierarchy of their affiliates at an accelerated pace, often beyond the true potential of the individuals involved.

- Develop an export base in a less-developed country, although alternative supply sources may be preferable.

- Introduce comprehensive social-benefits programs—full-day feeding, day-care centers, and medical benefits to employees and their dependents—well in advance of national mandates.

These represent just a few ways in which MNCs may rationalize their viability objectives in order to enhance their legitimacy in developing countries. And, we expect that these methods will be of increasing importance.

Host governments, in return, must provide a positive investment climate: political stability plus proper economic incentives to foreign investors. Whatever their ideological leaning, emerging nations openly concede the value of attracting overseas investment. Only recently, for instance, capital-starved Chile severed its ties with the hostile Andean Pact—announcing that aggressive policies against foreign investors were self-defeating. Despite the checkered profile of some multinational corporations within its borders, Chile's military government expressed its need for more receptive, less restrictive relations with potential investors from at home and abroad. Of course, the extent to which such directed governments lose favor with the local citizenry—because of the combination of oppressive home rule and special appeals to outsiders—remains unanswered.

Table 7.1 compares three primary patterns open to Third and Fourth World countries intent on economic development:[4]

Pattern I describes the ethnocentric approach to foreign investment in the developing world. In every important decision, MNCs attempt to unilaterally acquire permanent advantages over the host country.

Pattern II, by contrast, shifts the dominant role to local stakeholders. Restrictive legislation—including phase-out provisions—confront MNCs doing business in these countries.

Pattern III reflects the integrative-geocentric approach to economic development. Key stakeholders in the host country express a willingness to involve outsiders in the industrialization process. *Selective* interdependence is openly acknowledged by MNCs and developing nations.

Whatever the final choice, the challenge of the private and public sectors in developing nations is to understand their mutual areas of

Table 7.1
Approaches to Economic Development

	Pattern I	Pattern II	Pattern III
1. Equity	No local equity required or permitted.	Local ownership required or fade-out formula.	Equity in parent corporation encouraged or equity in GISC networks of connections with other countries.
2. Local content	Low local content requirements. No import licensing.	Very high local content requirements, regardless of cost. High import licensing.	Local content requirements in areas of worldwide capabilities, or GISC requirements. Labor-intensive when appropriate.
3. Profit and royalty remittance controls	Few profit and royalty remittance controls.	Very high profit and remittance controls.	Planned and equitable profit and royalty remittance patterns as part of firm or GISC.
4. Personnel restrictions	No personnel restrictions. Foreigners favored.	High personnel restrictions. Foreigners excluded.	Planned personnel exchanges with upgrading of local personnel to worldwide standards or GISC standards.
5. Expropriation and nationalization	Little or no expropriation or nationalization.	Aim to expropriate and nationalize all large foreign companies' holdings.	Distinguish core industries from worldwide industries in which host country has a stake.

Table 7.1 cont'd.

	Pattern I	Pattern II	Pattern III
6. Borrowing restrictions	Foreign firms borrow heavily locally.	Foreign firms bring capital in, then "fade out" or divest.	Plan reciprocation of local and foreign borrowing activities (local firms borrow in parent country), or in terms of GISC potentialities.
7. Tax discrimination	Tax incentives for foreign firms.	Foreigners more heavily taxed.	Foreign and domestic firms taxed equally.
8. Acquisition	Few or no barriers to acquisitions of any local firms by foreign MNCs.	All acquisitions by foreign firms barred from local takeovers.	Acquisitions permitted if worldwide capability planned or a GISC connection included.
9. Investment and incentive barriers	Incentives for investment very high. Few or no barriers.	Investment and incentives considered barriers to foreign investment.	Incentives for foreign firms to create worldwide centers of excellence, with local spinoffs which become parts of GISCs.
10. Demand for exports	Little or no demand for exports.	High demand for exports, regardless of competitiveness.	Demand for exports of specialized products as part of firm or GISC.

Source: Howard V. Perlmutter, "The Multinational Corporation: Decade One of the Emerging Global Industrial System," in Said and Simmons, eds., *The New Sovereigns* (New York: Prentice-Hall, 1976).

interest, and to capture the benefits of corporate investment without its costs.

The social, political, and economic realities of today and tomorrow suggest that multilateral linkages between internal and external stakeholders will play an increasingly important role. In this regard, various social-architectural approaches to collaborative problem solving apply. Let us turn to one important application.

INTEGRATED AREA DEVELOPMENT (IAD)

The concept of integrated area development was first proposed in 1976 by prominent Filipino industrialist and educator Sixto Roxas.[5] The setting was the Singapore meetings of the Pacific Forum, an organization of leading Asian and American businessmen and public officials. By providing a context for the constructive and creative exchange of views on important policy issues in the Pacific Basin, the Forum was instrumental in helping to clarify and promote greater understanding of integrated approaches to economic development in Asia.

Designed to alleviate the all-too-familiar problems of rural economic development, IAD views the human community as the principal beneficiary of progress. The notion is based on the idea that the source of livelihood for communities in Asia must come from villages around market towns, which will serve as the primary economic systems of the future. In addition, the sources of rural livelihood must eventually be shared by agricultural and nonagricultural industries.

The IAD process is characterized by the following:

• *A "total-systems" orientation.*   This comprehensive framework of analysis requires that the critical interdependencies of all elements within the region be considered. Concern and attention are simultaneously placed on the welfare of the local citizenry, natural surroundings and resources, economic realities, technological advantages, and financial opportunities.

The total-systems concept can be contrasted with the more traditional "linear" approach to economic development, where a multinational enterprise enters a region exclusively in search of market opportunities in its major area of business activity, with limited concern for the socioeconomic environment. Predictably, important questions of community development often remain unanswered, and this one-sided commitment leads to an imbalance in the area's maturation, with the host government forced to assume the principal responsibility of serving community needs. At best, involvement by the private sector under the linear scheme is confined to charitable contributions and tax payments.

Conversely, the total-systems approach attempts to identify areas of mutual interest between indigenous citizen groups and potential investors prior to the initiation of a project. It represents an important social-architectural application to economic betterment. Common problems and solutions are jointly articulated, and the total developmental effort is thereby enhanced.

• *A core project in a traditional industry.* Most frequently, agribusiness is the selected point of departure, and this provides the foundation for the IAD project. Next come satellite businesses (marketing, distribution, and financial services) and infrastructure subsystems (roads, communications, schools, and the like); they complement the core industry. Finally, widespread industrial diversification takes place. Through this evolutionary process an integrated program emerges.

• *A prime contractor.* IAD is carefully planned and executed by a lead agency, usually private, with adequate and sufficient governmental support to ensure success of the project. The firm that oversees the development effort provides the necessary financial and managerial resources to direct the project from start to finish. But, in most cases, syndication of additional business firms is intended.

The overheads for planning and development are substantial, and these up-front costs are absorbed primarily by the prime contracting agency. However, some are shared by the host government, and these amounts—especially for infrastructure development—are determined through prior negotiation. Similarly, the specific allocations of overheads between the private and public sector should be delineated before the project is undertaken.

• *Systematic staging of operations.* Within the total-systems framework, IAD development is planned to evolve through four distinct phases:

1. *Subsistence phase.* The objective of the initial phase is simply to improve existing physical conditions within the areas

toward increasing productivity in agriculture, the natural entry point for development. Among the measures immediately required might be the eradication of infectious disease, swamp reclamation, and the construction of dams and reservoirs.

2. *Income-earning phase.* With the completion of first-phase projects, it is envisioned that farmers' incomes will have been raised substantially. It now becomes feasible to supplement the building of physical infrastructure with the provision of agricultural inputs—credits, seeds, fertilizers, tools and implements, and investments in human capital. At this point, additional income-generating projects may also be promoted, such as vegetable gardening, livestock raising, and cottage industries, to offset the limited earnings of farmers from small landholdings.

3. *Investors phase.* After the second-phase projects, incomes in the region should have risen to such a level that surplus earnings can now be set aside as savings. On the sociocultural side, the value of budgeting, organization, and cooperative action should have been implanted among the population. The farmers now participate as part owners in such projects as the feed mill, agricultural equipment and motor pool, processing facilities, and others. Consequently, investable funds in the community become involved in the risk-taking and profit-making aspects of income-generating projects.

4. *Managers phase.* With the foundations for rational development in place, residents of the area are now prepared to take full control over the various enterprises in the region. This final period is characterized by the gradual phasing out of external agencies in the development process, but with the host government continuing to serve the residents with broad guidance and advice.

A conceptual description of the role transformation process accompanying these phases is shown in Fig. 7.1.

Therefore, IAD is designed to build a viable human settlement on a strong socioeconomic foundation. But even when development reaches the majority of a community, special problems arise, for, as Erich Fromm has observed, alienation in wasteful affluence is no less dehumanizing than alienation in misery.[6]

True development comprises not only certain benefits but also their modes of access and distribution. How these benefits are

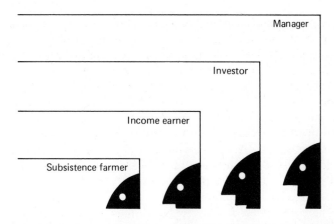

Fig. 7.1 Role transformation process. (From Victor M. Ordoñez, "Bancom's Operational Model for Countryside Development in Southeast Asia," Unpublished Working Paper, Bancom Institute on Development Technology, Manila, February 1977.)

obtained and whom they reach are vital questions. Thus, if rapid industrialization or increased food production are gained not through mobilizing incentive systems of the population or harnessing new entrepreneurial energies but via dictatorial terror, the result is not genuine development. Or, if landless peasants, oppressed by feudalistic landlords, struggle to win an agrarian reform only to discover later that they have simply changed masters—from a land-owning patron to a faceless state technocrat—nothing genuinely developmental has taken place. In short, *how* gains are made is as important as *what* is gained.[7]

The Sab-a-Basin Project

The initial pilot attempt at integrated area development recently began in the Philippines' central island-province of Leyte. The designated area, Sub-a-Basin, covers more than 300,000 acres of low-lying plains, almost 10 percent of which is swampland. Its total population is approximately 340,000 and 47 percent of the work force derives its income from agriculture.

Although great potential exists for fishing, forestry, and diversified agribusiness, the area is economically depressed and underdeveloped. Existing patterns of poverty within the Basin are traceable to such ecological and economic factors as low agricultural productivity, land erosion and flooding, as well as inadequate infrastructure and limited technical skills. The presence of infectious diseases, principally schistosomiasis, in the Basin aggravates these conditions.

Through a presidential decree, the Sab-a-Basin Development Authority was formed to introduce IAD projects to the area. The principal participants were the National Grains Authority, the Governor of Leyte, and, from the private sector, Bancom Farm Services Corporation. As prime contractor, the latter organization is obliged to provide all necessary technical expertise and to help raise the needed project funds. (It is a subsidiary of Bancom, the largest merchant bank in the Philippines.)

The core project is water resource management, aimed at converting the Basin's swamplands into productive grain farming. Special attention is directed toward large-scale rice production, using light and medium equipment for farm mechanization.

Ancillary projects also include a manpower training program designed to educate farmers and out-of-school-youths in rice and grain-production techniques; a seed-production program for screening varieties best suited to the Basin's conditions; and production of these seeds in quantities sufficient to supply the area's needs. The plans also consider much-needed infrastructure developments: road and transportation networks, irrigation systems, utilities, and a motorpool.

In the area of social services, a few representative projects to be implemented include:

1. *Education and manpower training.* Undertaken in cooperation with the Department of Education and Culture, the educational program will have two aspects: a formal education system with its general and vocational components and adult education, and a manpower training program for agriculture and industry. The latter will encompass practical training in rice production, farm-implement operation and maintenance, and an integrated rice-production training program.

2. *Health.* The rural health unit to be established in each municipality will engage in such activities as primary health-care services, referrals, home visits, immunization, and emergency treatment. It will offer preventive, curative, and rehabilitative health care, including the

expansion of present public-health facilities, training of paramedics and "barefoot doctors," family planning, and general health education.

3. *Housing.* The housing program will use indigenous materials and labor to minimize costs. Cluster-type settlement layouts will be followed, with ample yard space for vegetable gardening, livestock, and poultry raising. These consolidated villages will promote better interaction among neighbors as well as assure community security.

The interrelationships between the major components in this first IAD project are described in Fig. 7.2.

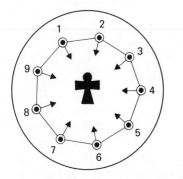

1. Water resource management
2. Swamp-upland development
3. Compact farming
4. Coconut intercropping and replanting
5. Livestock and poultry development
6. Fisheries production
7. Agro-industrial development
8. Infrastructure
9. Social services

Fig. 7.2 Major components of IAD program. (From Victor M. Ordoñez, "Bancom's Operational Model for Countryside Development in Southeast Asia," Unpublished Working Paper, Bancom Institute on Development Technology, Manila, February 1977.)

Although the Sab-a-Basin effort is still in its initial stages—at this writing, only two years into operation—the results have been impressive. Already, for example, over one-third of the swampland has been reclaimed for active crop growing; similarly, significant headway has been made in infrastructure development and improvement of social services.

THE HONOLULU FORUM

A second session of selected Pacific Forum members and academics met in Honolulu in April 1977 to explore in depth barriers to the implementation of integrated area development. To a degree, participants considered the progress of the Sab-a-Basin pilot project. More generally, however, the focus was on the strategic aspects of total-systems development and its potential applicability to other emerging nations of the Pacific Basin. The central findings and comments of these meetings are summarized below.

Cost, Risks, and Payoffs to Private Investors

Business investments are made on a competitive basis. With scarce resources to allocate, investors carefully compare all possible business opportunities at home and abroad. Particularly when IAD ventures in developing countries are concerned, corporate shareholders must be firmly convinced that the benefits exceed the costs. Add to this the incremental costs of infrastructure development, and the task of building foreign-investor interest in integrated projects becomes much more difficult.

Admittedly, this added cost and its risks represent nothing new to many industries: petroleum, primary metals, and the like. MNCs in these industries have long been accustomed to investments in social overhead—harbor dredging, road construction, telecommunications, and so forth. But, for other industries, this will require special convincing. Unlike the oil industry, the economic dynamics of less capital-intensive industries may make it prohibitive for one or even a few companies to carry the costs of infrastructure development.

Related, too, is the timing problem of IAD projects. The critics argue that the total-systems concept may be too futuristic. Such proposals, they note, work only for investments with extended time horizons of seven to twenty years: petroleum, mining, and very few others. At the same time, they grudgingly admit that companies in these very industries experience the greatest threat of government reprisal. Therefore, they are the ones who can most benefit from the integrated development approach.

Nevertheless, even IAD's proponents agree that evaluating investments in developing countries beyond five years causes problems for corporate decision makers. At the very least, participating companies need special assurances of political stability, capital adequacy, and related concerns.

Then there is the problem of investors' venturing outside their traditional business lines to establish the ancillary businesses and infrastructure needed to support the core activity in crop growing, fishing, or the like. Not only are the capital requirements staggering, but the companies are also being asked to walk on uncertain ground. Unlike the familiar forms of linear development, IAD, at the very least demands a higher level of commitment and expertise from interested investors. When compared to the other investment opportunities available to the firm, these additional costs and risks must be offset by a higher rate of return. Needless to say, the potential gains of IAD projects, such as Sab-a-Basin, have to be clearly articulated to the investment community.

No doubt, the rising corporate concern for legitimacy as well as profitability in developing countries may provide the answer. Enlightened investors are beginning to realize the inevitability of their assisting in infrastructure and related industrial developments. To survive, grow, and remain profitable in the Third and Fourth Worlds means greater corporate involvement in these once-alien sectors. Ongoing contributions of this variety will legitimatize the enterprise in the host country; and only through demonstrating its indispensability to the local community can the firm's long-term viability be ensured.

In terms of the bottom line, the payoff of social-architectural involvements is greater investment security and reduced exposure to political risk. The apparently high costs and risks of integrated area development may also be minimized by sharing them with other investors and the host government.

Syndication

Integrated area development means a multiproject approach to economic development. Besides reducing the risks of any single investor, a strong coalition of diverse businesses can provide the financial and managerial resources needed to move such a bold undertaking to completion.

But like any marriage, the shared strategy of IAD may suffer stress and strain. For the initial investor, the prime contractor in such a syndication, the risks are highest. Pulling together interested domestic and foreign investors at various points in time takes considerable effort, and few firms today have either the experience or the expertise to accomplish this successfully. For example, there is little guarantee that subsequent investors will be attracted to the project as it evolves through phases that require their special skills. Without their participation, the project will not succeed.

Then, too, there are the inevitable day-to-day conflicts of interest that are bound to occur once the project takes shape. The analogy of a domestic shopping-center development—while somewhat helpful— breaks down when dealing with complex socioeconomic development in an emerging Asian nation.

With syndication there is also the danger of fragmentation. Most important is the loss of important economies of scale; and, in many core industries, these are critical to the project's success. For instance, if numerous small farmers and several large producers are combined into a major agricultural project, many observers feel that such an effort—comprised of small-lot farming—may not be economically feasible. Therefore, careful consideration must be given to the economic limits of proposed coalitions.

Within these bounds, executives stress the importance of selecting the proper core industries for integrated area development. They cite agriculture, fishing, and mining as most ideally suited for the lead investment in a more comprehensive development plan. Not only do these integrated industries yield substantial primary and secondary expenditures, but also the levels of skills involved are within the capabilities of rural citizens. In addition, these industrial groups foster much-needed infrastructure development in processing, marketing, distribution, and financing.

Syndication would also best be served by avoiding start-up projects in remote and totally undeveloped rural areas. Businesspeople prefer to stage their investments in communities somewhat closer to the take-off stage of development and with some existing infrastructure. Hence, the consensus is that an existing venture in, say, coconut growing would be more attractive as the entry point for IAD than one in a completely impoverished community. Affiliation with an ongoing industry would also lessen the high risks associated with a more energetic program of economic development.

Role of the Host Government

Foreign investors agree that the success of integrated area development is dependent on the enlightened participation of the host government. Public officials must understand the risk-reward requirements of potential investors, since it is government which must oversee the negotiation process with interested businesses as well as community leaders. In so doing, the ground rules of IAD must be clearly communicated. Stated differently, the role of government—what it can and cannot undertake—must be fully understood *in advance* by all interest groups.

Domestic and foreign corporations considering long-term equity and management control in IAD projects would be wise to look elsewhere. Over time, rural residents are expected to assume expanded ownership and management responsibilities in the project. Under existing Philippine law, for example, gradual divestment must occur over a twenty-year period. Hence, participating firms must expect to phase down the equity portions of their investments.

Here, of course, government can help. The timing of divestment must be spelled out in the initial agreements, and government should assume major responsibility in developing adequate capital markets for acquiring ownership of outside interests. (Experience to date indicates that foreign multinationals, at least in the Philippines, have been able to sell their investments at rather attractive prices.)

So, too, for managerial transitions. Control must pass to resident managers according to some agreed-on timetable. As with equity control, the details must be mutually established in the initial contract.

Furthermore, multinational companies interested in land ownership should also avoid IAD projects. Given the sensitivity of the local populace for control over their own natural resources, governments must safeguard these basic rights. In all instances, title for land parcels remain with the local residents.

Beyond the especially sensitive areas of ownership and management control, foreign investors should expect certain assurances from the host government. First, the social overheads associated with IAD should not be the exclusive burden of private investors. From its tax revenues, government assumes a legal obligation to provide a comprehensive network of social and economic services. To be sure, corporations should be willing to share the load, but on an equitable basis. Considerable attention, therefore, must be given to government's expectations of private-sector contributions to infrastructure development. We would expect, for example, that some infrastructure and ancillary areas—rural banking, credit and collection, and land-use planning—would be best undertaken by the public sector, while others—syndication, research and development, and managerial training—should be left in private hands.

Next, some system of market guarantees may be needed to attract the business community. Here, the utilities concept of a "franchise area" may be appropriate, with IAD investors given exclusive market rights and buffered from their major competitors. Also, it may be necessary for government to establish guaranteed prices for the goods and services produced in the rural area—at least until a solid track record has been established. Administered prices are especially important in agribusiness and related activities where severe seasonal and cyclical swings may be anticipated.

Related to restrained competition, particularly in the early years of operation, are possible tax incentives. Businesspeople keen on integrated development point to Puerto Rico's successful "Operation Bootstrap" campaign, which attracted over four hundred private investors. Special incentives, tax holidays, accelerated write-offs, and other features should be carefully explored by the host government. Along with a significant infusion of front-end capital by the public sector, these efforts could substantially reduce the high costs and risks of rural development.

Shared responsibility by the private and public sector demonstrate the need for efficient negotiations. Today, dealings with almost any government, developed or developing, can be an exercise in frustration. Traditional bureaucracies endanger any serious commitment to IAD. Proponents argue that host governments eager to implement such bold programs should appoint a single agency with exclusive bargaining powers. By identifying one spokesperson for the public sector, participating business can look forward to expeditious negotiations conducted in good faith. Anything more complex may seriously jeopardize IAD proposals.

Even efficient negotiations are meaningless without official assurances of political stability. True, no nation can predict with complete certainty the future course of events within its boundaries. Nonetheless, governments can adopt internal and external policies which are less likely to cause political upheaval; and a commitment to such a course should be made by the host government.

Similarly, the nation's present and future stance with respect to MNCs should be made explicit. Mutually agreed-on policies should be openly communicated regarding, for example, the arbitration process of disputes between foreign investors and the host government. Comprehensive programs designed to preserve political stability and to provide a favorable investment climate carry considerable appeal in corporate boardrooms.

Role of International Financial Institutions

Given the significant financial requirements of IAD, regional and international funding agencies must play an important role. As with other participating groups, they will have to be sensitized to the total-systems approach.

For historical convenience, most international financial institutions think in linear or project terms. However, in evaluating IAD programs—with their extended investment horizons, multiple participation, and mixed profit and nonprofit undertakings—new methods of program evaluation must be utilized. In this regard, private investors and host countries must appeal jointly to international agencies if supplementary funding is to be obtained.

Involvement of Local Residents

Acceptance and enthusiasm of the community for integrated projects are also essential. This is particularly important as the local citizenry gradually assume positions of responsibility as project investors and managers.

With their inevitable mistrust of the central government and the investment community, residents of rural communities expect more formal involvement in integrated area development. While notions of a renewable community franchise approved by public referendum may seem remote, both the private and public sectors are advised to explore innovative ways of building community support. Without it, IAD has only limited applicability.

Although still in its embryonic stage, the Sab-a-Basin development has won the support of those indigenous to the area. Importantly, fundamental control and ownership of the lands remains with the local populace, and new methods are being introduced by the private and public sector to increase agricultural productivity. As an example, a central tractor pool available to local farmers can be used to plow their own land parcels at nominal charges.

Accelerating the development of IAD residents from project employees to investors requires creative ways of encouraging capital accumulation at the grass-roots level. For the program to succeed, incremental income in the community must be funneled into savings, and this challenge should not be regarded lightly. Such a process must occur if adequate financial resources are to be made available as outside investors divest from the project.

Equally important is the need for the community to provide managerial resources for positions of increasing importance. Several observers feel that this may be the single most important constraint to the success of IAD. Accordingly, considerable attention must be given to the education and training of indigenous citizens with high management potential. As with the other areas, a collaborative response by private- and public-sector participants may provide the answer.

Limitations aside, the general consensus of the Honolulu sessions was supportive of the integrated area development concept. Rather than interpreting greater public intervention in the development process as "creeping expropriation," business leaders viewed as inevitable the need for a total-systems approach. On balance, it was agreed that IAD offers both the private and public sectors an opportunity to participate meaningfully in improving the economic well-being of Asian nations.

The concerns registered in Honolulu were published in monograph form and disseminated to a wide range of interested parties.[8] Consequently, this document set the agenda, "A Positive Strategy for Foreign Investment," for a third meeting of the Pacific Forum in the Philippines.

THE MANILA FORUM

Held four months after the Honolulu Forum, the Manila sessions tended to move influential investors and government leaders closer to the point of ratification of integrated area development. While white papers representing many diverse viewpoints were presented, consensus began to emerge over the course of this five-day round of meetings. Most important, participants agreed on an idealized form of development. They were able to establish, for example, more realistic timetables for syndication, foreign divestment, and role transformation of the rural community.

This level of agreement would not have occurred without a visit by Forum participants to Sab-a-Basin. While there, executives were able to view both the problems and progress of this initial demonstration project. As on-site observers, they were better equipped to modify the somewhat more utopian, earlier versions of integrated area development to achieve an idealized form of total-systems development, endorsed by the majority of the Forum.

Planners of the change process emphasize the importance of seeking such an idealized state. "Interactive planning," as Russell Ackoff calls it, conceives of planning as the design of a desirable future and the invention of ways to bring it about.[9] Yet, an idealized design differs from a utopian design. In Ackoff's words: "To begin with, it [idealized design] does not pretend to be a perfect state. Rather, it is built on the realization that our concept of the ideal is subject to continuous change in light of new experience, information, knowledge, understanding, wisdom, and values. Furthermore, the designers engaged in idealization cannot answer all the questions they have about what the system ought to be. Therefore, they must design a capability for answering these questions experimentally. So it is an ideal-seeking system, unlike utopia which pretends to be beyond improvement."[10]

By moving IAD from a utopian framework to an idealized one, the Manila Forum made a significant contribution. Executives from the private and public sectors came away with an improved understanding of developmental targets and the methods of achieving them.

Taken together, the three Pacific Forum meetings induced a familiar process of attitudinal change[11]:

1. *Unfreezing* began in Pacific Forum I in Singapore, with change makers exposed to a rather dramatic, innovative concept of a collaborative approach to rural development in Asia. The legitimacy of the Pacific Forum itself and the credibility of the concept's creator, Sixto Roxas, provided sufficient sanction to reduce the initial skepticism of the total-systems approach.

2. *Changing* became visible in Pacific Forums I and II in Honolulu and Manila, respectively. Particularly in the latter sessions, consensus surfaced on the direction of change that will characterize future attempts at economic development. That private organizations would be expected to take the initiative in, say, infrastructure development—

once an alien notion—was accepted as not only inevitable but also desirable.

3. *Refreezing* is, at the time of this writing, in progress. For some, most noticeably those associated with other projects in the Philippines, substantial headway toward fuller acceptance of IAD has already occurred. But for others, the investment and attitudinal climates of their environments are not yet ripe for the level of commitment required to make the concept operational. Nonetheless, through subsequent meetings of the Forum, there will be ample opportunity to enable dissemination of the benefits of IAD cases to the nonaligned.

Integrated area development—in both theory and practice—is in its infancy. At the earliest, validation studies are still twelve to twenty-four months away. And whether the Philippines, given its potential instabilities, is the best point of departure, remains to be seen.

Nevertheless, IAD is attracting a broad base of interest from the emerging world. The Association of South East Asian Nations (ASEAN) and the United Nations Commission on Trade and Development (UNCTAD), two powerful institutions representing developing nations, are reviewing total-systems development for possible discussion in their upcoming meetings. With solidarity increasing among Third and Fourth World nations, it is clear that MNCs investing in developing countries will have to do so along integrated lines. What is not clear, however, is whether LDCs themselves will have the ability to sustain popular commitment and support such projects. Nevertheless, it is our opinion that the ultimate impact of IAD is likely to be quite profound.

SUMMARY

Economic change is a most critical aspect of modernization. With their limited resources, high illiteracy rates, low investment, and snowballing urban growth, developing countries are under great strain to appease their citizens' aspirations adequately. The race is not only against time. In societies where burgeoning populations compound the difficulty of achieving sustained economic growth, the race is with life itself.[12]

But any developmental effort in which there is no interchange of ideas, knowledge, and skills among cooperating cultures is doomed. The gains, if any, to the host country are ephemeral.

Integrated area development minimizes this danger by providing a permanent sharing at the community level. Indeed, such "community-building" aspects of international relations, Miriam Camps argues, far exceed the traditional "balance of power" issues.[13] The social-architectural perspective to community building in developing countries offers one approach to the problem.

NOTES

1. See, for example, Richard Barnet, *Intervention and Revolution* (New York: Institute for Policy Studies, 1972); Harry Magdoff, *The Age of Imperialism* (New York: Modern Reader Paperbacks, 1969); and *Multinational Corporations in World Development* (New York: United Nations Department of Economic and Social Affairs, 1973).

2. Richard J. Barnet and Ronald E. Mueller, *Global Reach: The Power of Multinational Corporations* (New York: Simon and Schuster, 1974).

3. Robert Wenkam, *The Great Pacific Rip-Off* (Chicago: Follett, 1974), p. 230.

4. Howard V. Perlmutter, "The Multinational Corporation: Decade One of the Emerging Global Industrial System," in Said and Simmons, eds., *The New Sovereigns* (New York: Prentice-Hall, 1976).

5. Sixto Roxas, "The Foreign Investment in Asia Pacific: A Suggested Framework for Regional Investment Policies," *The Economic and Political Growth Pattern of Asia-Pacific* (Honolulu: Pacific Forum Publications, 1976), pp. 103–124.

6. "Introduction" to Erich Fromm, ed., *Socialist Humanism* (New York: Anchor Books, 1966), p. ix.

7. Denis Goulet, "World Interdependence: Verbal Smokescreen or New Ethnic?" *ODC Development Paper 21* (Washington: Overseas Development Council, 1966), p. 11.

8. Marvin D. Loper and David A. Heenan, "Integrated Area Development: Myth or Reality?" *Pacific Forum Monograph Series*, Honolulu, June 1977.

9. Russell L. Ackoff, "The Corporate Rain Dance," *The Wharton Magazine,* Winter 1977, p. 39.

10. Ibid., p. 41.

11. See Edgar H. Schein, "Management Development as a Process of Influence," *Industrial Management Review*, May 1961.

12. Thomas A. Hiatt and Mark Gerzon, ed., *The Young Internationalists* (Honolulu: The University of Hawaii, 1973), p. 106.
13. Miriam Camps, "The Management of Interdependence: A Preliminary View," *Papers on International Affairs No. 4* (New York: Council on Foreign Relations, 1974), p. 9.

8
BUILDING GLOBAL UNIVERSITIES

A social-architectural approach to the building of a global university must begin with a global perspective of the educational system. The problems faced by universities in all parts of the world and their future directions can be estimated in much the same way that scenarios are built for the global industrial system and the global urban system. Thus, process consultants must urge their clients to identify the key changes in the global educational process, and encourage their understanding of the impact of these changes on the client university.

The legitimization of any institution as a global university cannot be made unilaterally by groups in one country. There must be recognition by universities in other countries of its global character, and some external linkages established on the basis of reciprocity. Thus, the members of any given university must not begin with such questions as: How can we become *the* global university? How do we go about co-opting resources from other universities around the world? Can we conduct some kind of massive brain drain? Rather, more fundamental questions for world-oriented universities should include:

- What shall be the mission of our university in the context of future global educational systems?

- What roles can we play that will be legitimized worldwide?

- On what strengths as a university can we build?

- With which foreign universities should we cooperate to build recognized centers of worldwide competence?

- What sources of support might we expect internationally to build such competence?

- How can our multinationalization process be integrated with the grass-roots constituencies of the area in which we live?

Applying our EPRG attitudinal orientation to some of the key parameters of the university, we can anticipate the major difficulties in building a geocentric university. As Table 8.1 indicates, if a geocentric profile were sought, the composition of the trustees, faculty and students, curriculum, and standards would have to be worldwide. Furthermore, the sources of financial support would have to be forthcoming from many different countries, as well as from international institutions. But it is far more likely that the trustees and, to a lesser degree, the faculty and students are from one country or region— given the nature of the state and federal support and the traditional relationship of the alumni to the university. Thus, the chances are greater that most universities are primarily ethnocentric, with some poly- and regiocentric capabilities (for example, in area studies).

Nonetheless, almost every major university maintains some connection with at least one foreign institution. So, the question is not whether a university is international or not, since in most instances there are at least links with other countries, but how multinational it is and in what areas.

For universities, the dual demands of social architecture—viability and legitimacy—are more clearly defined for their international ventures. Home rule, for the most part, predominates. And few universities have raised the question of multinationalization with the same degree of precision as that experienced by MNCs. With occasional exceptions, one does not find in today's universities any kind of coordinative planning mechanism established to understand the global educational processes and emergent global values regarding the transmission of knowledge and ideas.

As becomes clear in the case that follows, there are real constraints on any university located in one geographical setting that proclaims itself a global university. The fact that its facilities and personnel are all confined to one locale underscores its necessarily limited resources and dependency on local, state, and federal support. As long as the key stakeholders possess the ethnocentric point of view, it is hard to imagine why they would support building a global university.

Furthermore, there are very different concepts of internationalism within the university. There are those who view the compilation of area knowledge and the study of foreign cultures as the primary international role of the university. Conversely, there are others, usually in the professional schools, who associate internationalism with training foreigners in such skills as hospital management, agricultural research, and dam construction.

Quite often, both groups miss the important issue: What can we learn from other countries, and what can we teach other countries? Rather than focusing on reciprocity, most campus concern with internationalism is based on ethnocentric premises: What can we teach others regarding our solutions to problems in their countries?

In terms of the definitions we introduced earlier, the university's traditional concept of internationalism is enclave-geocentric, not integrative-geocentric. As a result, educators in a network seeking truth and knowledge are not inclined to integrate the true need of multinationalism to their constituents in the immediate environment.

This omission is highlighted in the case of the University of Hawaii, as state officials see little connection between the cosmopolitan mission of the university and local priorities in higher education. If the globalization process is to succeed, local authorities must come to understand what connections, if any, exist between the geocentric goals of the university and pressing local problems, such as health care, agricultural productivity, and the like.

Thus, the internationally ambitious university must temper and integrate its global mission with the needs of stakeholders at home and abroad.[1] This means that a coalitional perspective must replace today's co-optive, competitive orientation.

THE UNIVERSITY OF HAWAII CASE

State universities have traditionally seen their mission primarily in terms of the local constituency, which pays the bills and supplies most students. In many respects, public institutions have no other alternatives. And, as a consequence, universities in, say, Montana, Kentucky, and Colorado often become almost indistinguishable.

Table 8.1
Four Types of International Orientation
of Universities

	Ethnocentric	Polycentric	Regiocentric	Geocentric
1. Mission	Seek and teach knowledge and skills based on home-country experiences.	Seek and teach knowledge and skills relative to a variety of cultures and nations.	Seek and teach knowledge and skills based on a regional experience and orientation.	Seek and teach knowledge and skills based on a global experience and orientation.
2. Role	Seek educational roles with home country as primary context.	Seek educational roles based on linkages with selected other countries.	Seek educational roles in a regional context, e.g., Asia/Pacific.	Seek educational roles in a global context but linked to local needs.
3. Stakeholder orientation (alumni, trustees)	Primary orientation to expectations of stakeholders' home country.	Primary orientation to expectations of alumni and trustees with a country-by-country orientation, in selected areas.	Primary orientation to expectations of regional stakeholders in selected areas of competence.	Primary orientation to expectation of stakeholders worldwide in selected areas.

Table 8.1 *cont'd.*

	Ethnocentric	Polycentric	Regiocentric	Geocentric
4. Faculty	Faculty recruited primarily from home country with home-country standards.	Faculty recruited from selected countries in various domains/area studies.	Regional recruitment of faculty by regional standards.	Globally recruited on worldwide standards and competence.
5. Students	Students recruited mainly from home country.	Students recruited on quotas from various countries.	Students recruited on a regional basis on merit.	Students recruited on a global basis on merit.
6. Curriculum	Course curriculum oriented to home country.	Course curriculum "comparative" in character.	Course curriculum based on regional orientation and perspective.	Course curriculum with global context and perspective.
7. Sources of financial support	From home country, private and public.	From different countries through partnerships, private and public.	From regional and local institutions, private and public.	From local, national, international institutions in advanced, developing, and socialist countries.

Source: Howard V. Perlmutter, "Concepts of the University in the Context of an Emerging Global Educational System," mimeographed (Philadelphia: Multinational Enterprise Unit, The Wharton School, University of Pennsylvania, 1976).

To avoid becoming "the University of Montana with a suntan," administrators and faculty at the University of Hawaii have long recognized their unique geographical and cultural advantages in international education. Under a master plan of "selective excellence," international studies receive special priorities in resource allocation, faculty recruitment, and the like.

Since the mid-1950s when this commitment to internationalism began, the results have been impressive. Today, the University of Hawaii offers more courses in Asian languages and studies than any other university in the world. Its library collection of Asian-related titles ranks fourth nationally. Over 1,500 foreign students from the Pacific Basin bring their rich and diverse backgrounds to the classroom. Perhaps most important, the prestigious East-West Center dominates the university's main campus at Manoa.

This track record, while impressive, is misleading. Most of the internationalism, for example, has been rather narrowly confined to several departments and colleges. Lack of a system-wide understanding and commitment, university leaders feel, seriously inhibits the institution's ability to become the educational leader in the study of Asia and the Pacific.

The International Task Force

In September 1975 the university president appointed a task force "to survey the extent and depth of our international activities—in research, teaching, and cooperative programs—and to come up with proposals on where the University should go as an international institution over the next five and ten years." Composed of role innovators from both the faculty and administration,[2] the task force had two distinct phases:

I. *Diagnosis* to assess the meaning of internationalism for the university and to present a proposed plan of action to the president. Here, the focus was almost exclusively internal with minimal participation of groups outside the university system.

II. *Implementation* to effect the recommendations of phase I. Particular emphasis was to be given to the university's external constituents, especially legislators and potential funding agencies.

Each phase was to last twelve months, and task-force membership in phase II was to be modified to include nonuniversity representatives.

Shortly after its appointment, the task force surveyed a sample of 300 faculty and administrators on several of the university's campuses. Most helpful in this process was a force-field-analysis questionnaire designed to surface sentiment on the strengths, weaknesses, and direction of the institution's international programs. External and internal driving and restraining forces affecting the university's present level of international competence were identifield. The results are summarized in Figs. 8.1 and 8.2.

Next, in-depth interviews were conducted with many of the questionnaire respondents as well as others. Follow-up discussions were also held with interested departments and schools. In addition, the task force laboriously investigated successful and unsuccessful attempts to internationalize other educational institutions.

After several months' study, the task force submitted its findings to the president and the greater university community. Its central conclusion: If the University of Hawaii were to become a first-rate state university, it must *first* become a leading international university. Specifically recommended was a full-scale effort to become the most prominent university in the Pacific Basin. But for this to happen, the task force contended, several "critical factors for success" would be required.

Extracted from the task-force report are these critical factors:

1. *Legislative and community support.*   As a state university, the university must secure the ongoing support of the state legislature and community for its international programs. Only with their backing can budgetary and nonbudgetary assistance for international education be assured. Before financial support can be forthcoming, these groups must sense the critical role of international education to the university system. Yet in the eyes of the task force and of most faculty, there is a strong perception that the state legislature and its constituency are not committed to internationalism.

Many faculty surveyed pointed to increasing parochialism by legislators, with top priority attention given only to those programs having a heavy "local" flavor. Others noted the growing level of provincialism in the community at large. While possibly some of these fears were unfounded, that most faculty considered them to exist was significant.

Nevertheless, most respondents felt that a significant potential exists in Hawaii for internationalism. The state's attractive mid-Pacific location and multiethnic heritage make the study of interna-

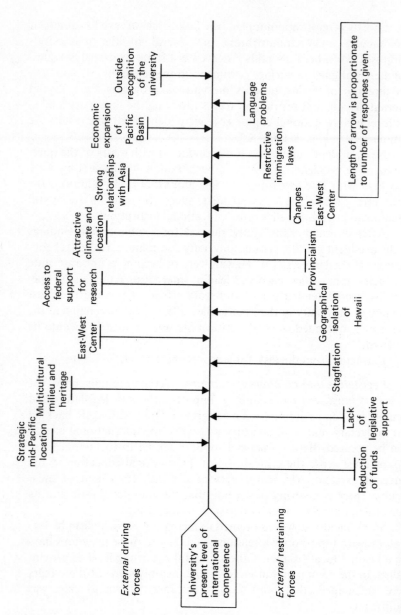

Fig. 8.1 Force-field-analysis A.

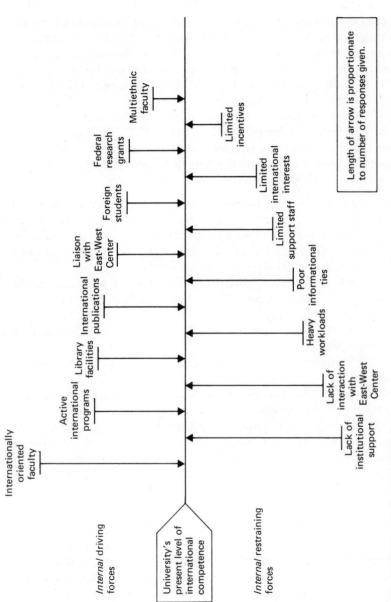

Length of arrow is proportionate to number of responses given.

Fig. 8.2 Force-field-analysis B.

tional affairs logical for the university to pursue. In addition, there are strong ties in the local community with the Pacific. Governmental agencies, business groups, and related institutions maintain an active presence in Asia. Private corporations, too, have developed a multinational profile in the Pacific. These trends can be expected to continue, and the university must keep pace.

Still, a wide gap exists between town and gown over the meaning and significance of international programs to higher education. For the university to achieve greatness as a state institution, it must communicate more effectively to the state the major educational and technical benefits of internationalism.

2. *Adequate financial support.*   As a corollary, only a closer bond between the university and the state can yield necessary financial support. Without adequate funding, first-rate international activities cannot survive. Given the isolated location of Hawaii, the need for overseas travel and field research is especially acute.

A review of funding patterns for international programs reveals that the most funds are provided by federal souces. While the university's record at securing federal funds is excellent (nationally, it ranks 32nd), the economic pinch is starting to take effect and these funds are becoming tighter.

If the state desires international excellence from its university, it must take the primary responsibility in supporting the international thrust of the university. Federal support, while welcome, should only supplement state support.

Other state funds—from the private sector—can also be solicited more actively. The task force noted that the University of Hawaii Foundation had taken a more aggressive stance in recent years and that is should be used more effectively to secure discretionary funds from private corporations with major business interests in the Pacific Basin.

3. *Internal commitment to internationalism.*   In the university system, there is a cadre of competent globalists. The faculty's excellence in international affairs is most often associated with Asian studies and languages, but, in many instances, it runs deeper. Virtually every academic unit on campus has at least one competent internationalist; most have more. More important, these men and women possess considerable field experience in Asia, which has enriched their academic backgrounds and professional interests.

Conversely, many other members of the university community feel excluded. For them, internationalism connotes something foreign or alien. Oftentimes, hostility or, at the very least, misunderstanding results. Nowhere does this seem to be more the case than in the central administration.

For the most part, the university administration is not viewed as being supportive of internationalism. Many faculty members sense an overall ambivalence or, even worse, negativism with respect to international programs. Shortsightedness and failure to consider the long-term perspective are administrative failings often mentioned by the faculty. Even more critical is the administration's apparent lack of clarity in policy making and direction regarding international affairs. There is growing concern that, in fact, the university is not committed to becoming a leading international university. For example, although Asian studies have been designated for "selected excellence," it is nowhere clearly stated that this area is to receive preferential treatment when resources are allocated. More often than not, when resources are scarce, these activities are the first to be cut back.

Further, international programs are coordinated in a sporadic and unsystematic manner. Even within Asian studies, resources are scattered across various departments and units. For example, College A may be anxious to launch a joint program in Indonesia with a local university—unaware that a firm relationship already exists between another UH College and a local university. Frequently, wasted effort and duplication result. Also questioned is the ability of a single department to go it alone internationally over time without borrowing from the competence of the rest of the university. In addition, there is a lack of interaction with the East-West Center.

Thus, the need exists for a university-wide coordinating office—well staffed and well funded—to oversee all international programs. A university truly committed to internationalism should have such a capability.

4. *Appropriate faculty support.*   Greater financial support and commitment by the administration for the university's international activities will go a long way toward improving faculty morale. Most needed are funds to attend scholarly conferences, to support working papers, to provide graduate assistance, and for other important projects. There is also strong consensus that heavy teaching and service workloads leave very little time for the faculty to engage in interna-

tional activities. With the current budget constraints, there are few opportunities for faculty to undertake international research.

More generally, there are few incentives in the present system to encourage the faculty's international involvement. Besides the frustrations of reduced travel assistance, UH professors point to the problems involved in their participating in meaningful overseas assignments. Extended leaves of absences or paid sabbaticals are almost impossible to come by. Others argue that their promotion and tenure opportunities are jeopardized when they accept foreign assignments. "Out-of-sight" apparently means "out-of-mind"—to the detriment of an individual's professional career. As a result, many have elected to stay in Hawaii to avoid the perils of an international experience.

Limitations aside, the university has assembled a group of leading international scholars in a relatively short time. With the proper backing, this faculty can achieve academic leadership in East-West education.

5. *Diverse student base.*   To be a leading international institution requires an internationally oriented student body. The diversity of UH students, particularly at the graduate level, has added significantly to the present level of international competence of the university. There is strong consensus that higher levels of qualified non-American students will accelerate the university's internationalization. Conversely, restrictive quotas that discriminate against nonresident students severely limit UH's global presence.

In addition to a diverse student body, there is also a need for appropriate student services. Problems ranging from summer employment to immigration affect all international students. Comprehensive student services are needed to make the university an attractive learning environment for students with multicultural backgrounds.

6. *Improved relations with the East-West Center (EWC).*   As a most unique institution, the Center has done much to strengthen UH's bid for international recognition. By providing training opportunities for foreign students and advanced scholars, the EWC enhances the worldwide stature of the university. Most of its relationships with the university are a distinct plus.

However, UH faculty feel that there has generally been poor coordination between the two institutions, to the overall detriment of the university. Moreover, there is considerable anxiety over the recent separation of the Center. For many, this means a likely reduction in degree-seeking students for the university with a consequent blow to its internationalism. For the university to take advantage of this globally recognized, federally funded institution requires a much clearer articulation of the relationship between these two institutions.

7. *First-class physical resources.* The university can take some pride in the modest facilities that have been committed to international education. Most often, UH's excellent library facilities are praised by faculty members. The Asia collection, in particular, is one of the most important collections of its kind anywhere in the world. Still, much more can be done—especially in the area of library support personnel. At the present time, a shortage of qualified manpower coupled with space constraints prevent more complete utilization of the library by faculty and students.

Likewise, language resources merit a higher level of university support. Excellent laboratory facilities, if given greater staffing assistance, could serve a broader base of the community. It would not take much to develop clear leadership in Asian and Pacific languages at the university.

While secondary in importance to faculty resources, these bricks-and-mortar aspects of the university's internationalization should not be understated. Physical facilities are visible and tangible. They signal to the world the university's true commitment to a particular educational objective.

8. *Effective relationships with external agencies.* For the university to achieve educational leadership in the Pacific, it must have meaningful links with the appropriate international agencies and institutions. Fortunately, national and international activities have supported various UH programs: overseas study, student exchanges, postdoctoral fellowships, and the like. For UH's international progress to be assured, this record of success must continue.

In addition, the university receives a steady stream of requests for technical and consulting assistance from foreign countries. Whether it be curriculum design for a fledgling School of Public Health or a geodetic survey, there are significant opportunities for the university's expertise. This should increase over time.

Firsthand overseas experiences have left UH with a strong core of international competence on campus. Still, many feel that there should be more effective coordination of these overseas activities.

What could formerly be handled adequately on an ad hoc basis deserves a higher level of professional administration.

The task force argued that, by heeding these eight critical factors, the university could enhance significantly its internationalization. Simply stated, this meant a more complete exploitation of Hawaii's natural locational and multicultural advantages.

Progress to Date

Since the task force's submission of the phase I report, the results have been unimpressive. The president's office withheld implementation of the report, and phase II of the project has been postponed indefinitely. In the words of one observer, "The Task Force on International Relations . . . worked diligently and devotedly in 1975–1976 to reassess the university's role and international institutions, only to have their report virtually ignored."

What went wrong? Factionalism, among other things, contributed to the lack of sucess of this change program.

Quite early in our diagnosis, it became clear that "internationalism" carries two rather distinct meanings on campus, as interpreted by two distinct groups:

1. *The academic internationalists'* claim to internationalism takes the form of scholarship and teaching in courses that, by definition, have a strong international orientation: Japanese languages, comparative political systems, ethnomusicology, and the like. They are represented almost exclusively by traditional departments in the College of Arts and Sciences.

2. *The administrative internationalists,* primarily located in the professional schools and colleges, oversee a variety of international programs—ranging from federal contracts to train doctors in Okinawa to exchange programs with leading Asian universities. Also included are on-campus programs to promote internationalism: study-abroad efforts, foreign-student counseling, and informational exchanges between professed internationalists.

Members from both groups were represented in the task force. In addition, both groups endorsed the central findings of the phase I report—with one noticeable exception. In its recommendations, the task force proposed one central agency, headed by a Vice President for International Affairs, to coordinate all international activities within the JH system. The administrative internationalists, in particular, sought to combine their widely scattered programs under a new structure—the Center for Asian and Pacific Studies (CAPS)—proposed (ironically) by the academic internationalists. The latter group, on the other hand, wanted to avoid contamination of CAPS by non-academic service units and, hence, preferred a scholarly enclave of Asiaphiles.

Much time and effort was consumed in attempting to reconcile these differing organizational philosophies. Inevitably, one task force member conceded, "It may be that this problem is insolvable in terms of a single institution framework." And, at the time of this writing, it appears that two separate agencies—CAPS and an international coordinating unit—may eventually be endorsed.

To the internal and external communities, however, these stops and starts have been costly. As one professor put it, "The situation at the university has vastly deteriorated. It's tragic because it's happening when world attention is shifting to the Pacific."[3]

A more scathing criticism was offered by long-time internationalist and East-West Center director George M. Kanahele: "It is the irony of ironies that as the world turns toward the Pacific Era, we seem to be turning away from it. As a state, we seem to have lost sight of the fact that Hawaii has a role to play in the Pacific. Rapidly disappearing . . . is the reputation of the University of Hawaii as one of the great international institutions in the Pacific. The Peace Corps training program, the Asia Training Center, the Tropical Rice Production Center, American Field Services Program, Fulbright Orientation Program, and others have been dropped in recent years. Drastically curtailed are other activities including the Office of Foreign Contracts, the Study Abroad Program, and the Advisory Council on International Relations of the University of Hawaii, the major coordinating body of the state-wide system."[4]

Whether complacency or loss of vision, as Kanahele sees it, were the more fundamental causes for the task force's lack of success is difficult to assess. Only time will tell the extent of the university's true commitment to internationalism.

SUCCESS OR FAILURE IN MULTINATIONAL OD

By most standards, the University of Hawaii's attempt to build a more international university would be considered a failure. Conversely, the

Philippines' efforts in Sab-a-Basin to achieve agro-industrial development with the aid of MNCs have been relatively successful. By examining the underlying reasons for the success or failure of each case, process consultants can gain an in-depth understanding of the essential factors in any successful multinational OD program.

As a minimum, the social-architectural approach to international institution building must take into account six parameters—ranging from the form of internationalism to legitimacy considerations. Table 8.2 compares these dimensions for the Hawaii and Philippines cases, and a more complete discussion of each parameter follows:

1. *Kind of international orientation.*   Recall that integrated area development (IAD) began with the notion that self-help through local private- and public-sector involvements is an essential prerequisite to socioeconomic development in the Basin. Before external assistance from foreign-owned MNCs and international funding agencies could be obtained, change agents agreed that strong local or polycentric support—especially in infrastructure development—was needed. More-

Table 8.2

A Comparison of the Social-Architectural Approach to OD for Two Projects

Parameter	University of Hawaii	Philippines' Integrated Area Development
1. Kind of international orientation	Enclave-geocentric	Initially polycentric, later integrative-geocentric
2. Function of internationalization	Internationalization as an end	Internationalization as a means
3. Attitudes of state sponsors	Nonsupportive; considered obstacles	Are primary sponsors
4. Role of foreign stakeholders	Unclear definitions; role not legitimatized by local authorities	Defined and legitimatized by local authorities
5. Basis for viability	Home stakeholders dominate	Shared by home and foreign stakeholders
6. Basis for legitimacy	Home stakeholders dominate	Home stakeholders dominate, but with increasing involvement of foreign stakeholders

over, with their subsequent demonstration of a positive investment climate, the project's orientation began to shift from polycentrism to integrative-geocentrism. Sharing of IAD's costs and benefits began to be transmitted, at least in part, to external stakeholders.

International image building, so characteristic of enclave-geocentrism, dominated the University of Hawaii case. Here, the preoccupation was with becoming more cosmopolitan, but without any serious efforts to establish links with other Asian universities for the purpose of sharing resources and knowledge. Vague ideas of geographical adventurism led to serious conceptual misunderstanding amongst internal and external stakeholders over the proper international role of the university.

2. *Function of internationalization.*   As a corollary, the University of Hawaii viewed internationalism as a desired *end product.* In ideological terms, being more "international"—despite definitional confusion over its meaning—was a terminal stage, desirable for a university located in the middle of the Pacific Ocean.

By contrast, the Philippines considered internationalism as an instrument of economic development. The involved participation of foreign investors became a *means* of facilitating integrated area development. In this project, change agents were not convinced that internationalism by itself was worth achieving.

3. *Attitudes of state sponsors.*   In the Sab-a-Basin project, internal stakeholders expressed a positive attitude toward their internationalization. Moreover, they served as the prime movers, providing the core leadership and sponsorship for IAD.

Quite different attitudes existed for state sponsors in the University of Hawaii case. The central administration was viewed as nonsupportive of many campus groups. One faculty member commented, "Generally speaking, the administration has been more concerned with property than with international education, with pacifying the legislature than with providing international leadership." Distrust and suspicion of the state legislature were frequently cited. "Local emphasis is the major criteria for legislative support, and the legislature appears to be increasingly domestic in its orientation, at least in terms of fiscal support." Since, for the most part, state sponsors did not perceive any grass-roots benefits of internationalism, they were considered obstacles to the university's internationalization.

4. *Role of foreign stakeholders.* Local authorities in the Philippines were careful to establish an explicit and valuable role for outsiders in their development plans. Clearly articulated for foreign participation were such sensitive areas as equity and management control, land ownership, and technology transfers. Within these boundary conditions, the role of foreign stakeholders was legitimatized throughout the project.

Not so for the University of Hawaii. Here, the role of foreign universities and outside funding agencies was unclear. Certainly, there were no directed efforts to legitimatize their possible linkages with the university. For instance, proposals to award University of Hawaii degrees on foreign soil were soundly defeated.

5. *Basis for viability.*   For the Sab-a-Basin project to survive and grow beyond the pilot stage requires the participation of others outside the Philippines. MNCs and other external agencies offer much-needed managerial and financial resources. By the same token, outside institutions value the raw materials, market size, and strategic location that the Philippines offers their organizations. Thus, on both sides there are important incentives to build collaborative business ventures.

Again, the situation is quite different for the University of Hawaii. Almost 95 percent of its financial support is provided from state and federal funds. With the exception of Japan, Asian nations and their universities are perceived as a potential drain on already scarce resources. As a result, internationalization may decrease, not increase, the university's economic viability.

6. *Basis for legitimacy.*   As with the University's viability, local stakeholders heavily influence the degree to which its international plans are viewed as part of its core mission. To date, however, local constituencies receive higher priority than those from outside the state. This is likely to continue until change agents are able to demonstrate the potential benefits to the state of international linkages. But, for the immediate future, home stakeholders perceive serious attempts to internationalize the university as frivolous and without substance.

Granted, local stakeholders also dictate the extent to which IAD in the Philippines will be internationalized. Nevertheless, through the Pacific Forum sessions, there have been definite expressions of a willingness to accommodate the needs of foreign stakeholders, primarily

MNCs. As a trading nation with a rather limited spectrum of commodities and raw materials, the Philippines finds it in its best interests to continue to expand its international network. Within well-defined bounds, greater involvement of foreign investors should occur. Interdependence and indispensability, we expect, will emerge as a shared value of stakeholders at home and abroad.

CONCLUDING NOTE

The distinctions outlined above point to the difficulty in internationalizing social institutions, especially those in higher education. Longtime champion of international education, J. William Fulbright suggests: "We must try, through education, to realize something new in the world—by persuasion rather than by force, cooperatively rather than competitively, not for the purpose of gaining dominance for a nation or an ideology but for the purpose of helping every society develop its own concept of public decency and individual fulfillment.'"

Fulbright's challenge will require a social-architectural approach to multinational organization development. Restructuring higher education along global lines means bold new approaches aimed at involving foreign and domestic stakeholders in a systematic manner. Anything less is likely to generate cultural misunderstanding and lead to intellectual stagnation.

NOTES

1. Howard V. Perlmutter, "Concepts of a Global University in the Context of a Global Educational System," Working Paper (Philadelphia: Worldwide Institutions Research Group, The Wharton School, University of Pennsylvania, 1977).
2. Edgar H. Schein, "The Role Innovator and His Education," *Technology Review* 72: 33-37.
3. George S. Kanahele, "Hawaii's Pacific Role," *Honolulu Star-Bulletin,* 14 July 1977, p. A-21.
4. Ibid.
5. J. William Fulbright, "International Education: Focus for Corporate Support," *Harvard Business Review,* May–June 1977, p. 141.

9
A LOOK AT THE FUTURE

Throughout this book we have suggested that the traditional OD approach, which focuses on the single organization, is not enough. A social architectural perspective to multinational organization development—one that embraces not only external and internal stakeholders, but also multiorganizational needs—is required.

Similarly, Warren Bennis has argued that, "The main reason OD is in a cul-de-sac is because it is not looking at the right things. It is not looking at the environment sufficiently. It is not looking at the politics of what happens at the boundaries of organizations. It is not looking at the external factors."[1]

In our opinion, the environmental complexities of the organizations of today and tomorrow exist because of the network of diverse stakeholders who hold the solutions to international problems. No doubt, problems—international or domestic—require multiorganizational appreciation, collaborative planning, and cooperative interventions. Without these prerequisites, the legitimacy of any major change program will be jeopardized.

Multinational OD, then, means *multiorganizational development with a worldwide perspective.* This process, we expect, will have an increasing appeal for executives in organizations with global needs, as well as for OD practitioners eager to help them.

THE CONCEPT OF TURBULENCE

In the years ahead, new strategies will be needed to deal with the changing character of the transactional environment confronting worldwide institutions. Emery and Trist's concept of a "turbulent environment" best describes the global industrial system of today and tomorrow.[2]

This is what Daniel Bell had in mind when he put forth the proposition that "the nation-state has become too small for the big problems in life, and too big for the small problems."[3] Anticipating a rise in global uncertainty, Bell predicts somewhat less turbulence between employer and employee, but more between the MNC and external stakeholders. As the latter rise in importance, special problems are created for nation-states and their corporations.

In many countries, for example, stakeholder pressures have led to precarious coalition governments. In various ways, these governments attempt to compromise between the need for socioeconomic development and the increasing demands of companies, trade unions, and other stakeholder groups. For many nations, it is clear that solutions to the important problems of defense, health care, and education cannot be reached independently. Conversely, other nations are experiencing increasing pressure from local constituents to solve these problems at the local level. Interdependence or autarchy: this is the double bind that confronts governments around the world.

Many observers attribute the roots of this turbulence to major sociological and geopolitical transformations in our social structures. In advanced societies, the shift has been from a hierarchical, bureaucratic orientation to one of participation and egalitarianism. In other parts of the world, there has been a proliferation of nation-states, many with limited capabilities to manage their own destinies. Added to this are the significant technological advances that have heightened the potential for greater independence and have accelerated our transition to a postindustrial society.

This transformation, as Donald Schon has noted, has led to the loss of the stable state.[4] Readily visible today are new sources of turbulence in the stakeholder system. Whatever the institution, one sees:

• old stakeholders changing their former values;

- old stakeholders developing or acquiring more articulate spokespersons;
- old stakeholders seeking new bargaining power;
- new stakeholders emerging in importance;
- stakeholder contributions no longer linked with size or other traditional definitions of power;
- increased communication between stakeholders, with "snowballing" effects;
- coalitions among stakeholders, often leading to new instabilities.

Thus, it is no wonder that strategic planners use "turbulent"to describe the environment within which multinational institutions must operate. The only certainty, it seems, is future uncertainty.

It would perhaps be easiest simply to give in to this truism were it not for the high cost of doing so. Without question, MNCs of the future must adopt new skills to manage effectively under these conditions of turbulence. Let us now consider some new social-architectural approaches to managing at the global and organizational levels.

PROBLEMS AT THE GLOBAL LEVEL: THE RIO APPROACH

In the last decade, there have been several attempts at global modeling. The objective: to plot the likely course of future changes in the world environment. These projects, undertaken primarily by the Club of Rome, have evolved in both sophistication and focus.[5]

The Club's initial Forrester and Meadows models led to the popular book, *Limits of Growth,* which raised public consciousness of our planet's parameters in reconciling explosive growth in technology and population.[6] While these first-generation models of the world profoundly affected public awareness of "social limits" and the future of humankind, they were criticized for being overaggregated ("telling too much, but not enough"). Thus, in portraying the human condition as a whole, the creators of these models omitted such essential human elements as individual values, organizational structures, and the like.

Consequently, second-generation models were less aggregated and highlighted important regional distinctions: the developed versus less developed bloc, Latin America versus the United States, socialist versus market economies. In addition, more attention was given to the human side. These subsequent models took into account, for example, the notion that human pressures could disrupt the world system before natural pressures made themselves felt. Still, even these models centered primarily on physical and material "outer limits" rather than the "inner limits" of human perceptions, needs, and values.

To bridge this so-called "inner-outer gap," the Club of Rome launched a third-generation model in 1976. Headed by Nobel prize winner Jan Tinbergen, the Reshaping the International Order (RIO) Report now matches the outer insights provided by earlier studies with the inner dimensions of contemporary society. It compares what needs to be done with what people are willing to do.

The findings of the RIO report are detailed and cover a wide range of complex issues: reformation of the international economy, disarmament, "the brain drain," and others. The major conclusion, however, is that *a crisis of international structures* will be the challenge of future generations. "What is required is a new international order in which all benefit from change. What is required are fundamental institutional reforms, based upon a recognition of a common interest and mutual concern, in an increasingly interdependent world."[7]

Building New Social Institutions: The International Seabed Authority

In addition to reshaping existing international organizations, social architects will be called on to create *new* global structures. For example, with the growing importance of ocean resources, priority is being given to the establishment of an International Seabed Authority. Its major role would be to license MNCs to mine the high seas in areas beyond the 200-mile limit, where no nation has jurisdictional control.

Many unanswered questions stand in the way of such an agency: How should the wealth of the seas be divided between MNCs and nation states? How can a neutral authority be created, given the distrust between MNCs and developing nations? What sanctions could such an agency impose against MNCs or sovereign states? As a result, discussions of the International Seabed Authority are at an impasse, with different views being voiced by the following stakeholders:

• The mining consortia of MNCs that seek the freedom to mine the high seas, with all the prospects of financial success or failure.

• Nation-states engaged in land mining of manganese, nickel, cobalt, and copper—minerals competitive with the so-called "manganese nodules" found in abundance on the ocean floor. They want the power to control seabed production, in order to protect prices for minerals in their countries.

• Consuming countries, particularly those from the industrial world, eager to maintain continuous and reasonably priced supply sources of these important minerals.

• Mineral-poor, less-developed nations that seek some form of compensatory financing or redistribution of revenues from the consortia that mine these metals from the ocean.

The compromise, in theory at least, might be a parallel system that promotes active roles for these key actors as well as for the Authority. At the time of this writing, however, a workable agreement has not been reached.

In addition, private attempts to break the deadlock have been generally unsuccessful. Nevertheless, efforts to bring the delegates together in an informal setting without the restrictions of their official roles have created an improved climate for serious negotiations. Still, these activities have not been sufficient to produce an international treaty, and it is likely that each stakeholder will resort to unilateral action, with the deep-sea mining consortia simply going their own way.

Building such a new institution today seems a very difficult task. It may not be so elusive if change agents can answer the crucial question: What kinds of structures and learning processes can be set in motion in order to permit this kind of social architecture to take place? Practically speaking, the answer will require inviting key stakeholders to joint problem-solving sessions on specific issues, in the hope that more equitable and binding solutions can be reached. Moreover, success in the future means not only developing linkages between *existing* institutions, but also determining what *new* institutions are missing, how they should be established, and how they should be coordinated.

Managing Global Interdependence

How will these emerging interdependencies be managed? For the macroproblems confronting multilateral institutions, such as the United Nations, World Bank, and others, former ambassador and current director of the Aspen Institute's Program in International Affairs, Harlan Cleveland, advises that, "What seems to be required is a new kind of 'planetary bargain'—more accurately a collection of parallel bargains on such matters as food, population, energy, environment, money, investment, and security, in an unprecedented political bazaar."[8]

The notion of a "planetary bargain" has received considerable attention as an appropriate conceptual framework for coping with the evolving global ecology. Meeting recently in Berlin under the sponsorship of the Aspen Institute, a group of leading internationalists proposed a five-step process to deal with the macroproblems of today and tomorrow:[9]

1. *Preparation of a "solution."*   First, the problems must be defined, the subject matter organized, and sound policy responses or "solutions" presented. This solutions-first approach is totally consistent with Russel Ackoff's concept of "idealized redesign," mentioned earlier in this book. For Ackoff, solution building in the initial phases is "the most critical step in interactive planning." He suggests that "instead of planning *away from a current state,* we start planning *toward a desired state.* That means planning from the future to the present in contrast to conventional planning, which goes from the present to the future. The eyes of the planners are focused on ultimate objectives—ideals—throughout."[10]

For expediency reasons, this vital first step forward should be restricted to relatively few participants—fewer than in the later stages. Care, however, should be taken to minimize the perception of outsiders that specific policy outcomes have already been fixed by insiders. In fact, the solutions developed are tentative and essentially serve as policy benchmarks for subsequent stages in the change process.

2. *Prenegotiation.*   Next, broader participation is solicited, and an appropriate forum for discussion identified. Here the key question becomes: How do you get all the stakeholders in the act and still get some action?[11]

For global problems, a two-tier system of prenegotiation may work best. Initially, an ad hoc group of highly committed participants intimately works on a particular issue; then, their thoughts are presented to the wider international community for consideration. Under such a scheme, problems confronting the international monetary system, for instance, would only be forwarded to the International Monetary Fund *after* in-depth examination by a smaller, but more committed, group—in this case, the so-called "Group of 10" (major industrial countries).

Such a process of selective exclusion in the early stages of prenegotiation is highly efficient. And the costs of some potential alienation are more than offset by the benefits of avoiding marginally interested and even obstructive participants.

3. *Negotiation.*   Depending on the success of prenegotiation, this stage of the planetary bargain is usually confined to the few. In large groups, attempts to work out precise solutions—for example, the level of an import tariff on four-wheel-drive vehicles—tend not to work, except when formal caucuses succeed in breaking down negotiations into manageable segments.

4. *Ratification and legitimation.*   In this phase, the focus returns to expanded participation. Giving the larger international community a second attempt at what has been reworked by the core group will be necessary to legitimatize and, eventually, to effect implementation. Naturally, formal ratification through an acknowledged legal forum such as the United Nations General Assembly is ideal. Nonetheless, in many instances, suasion of world public opinion may be equally, if not more, potent. Witness, for instance, the rising global sensitivity to the issue of human rights, without any official legitimization.

5. *Operations.*   As with legitimization, implementation requires different process mechanisms and varies considerably from case to case. For example, if a binding worldwide agreement on air piracy is to be reached, universal involvement is virtually required. On the other hand, consensus on world coffee prices can be reached

through the few participating nations to the International Coffee Agreement.

On closer examination, this proposed format for planetary bargaining has, implicitly at least, been at work in resolving several macroproblems. One sees this in evidence in various issues relating to international trade, public health, aircraft hijacking, investment security, and other global problems. What is needed, therefore, is a comparable mechanism for handling the problems confronting MNCs.[12]

BRINGING THE STAKEHOLDERS INSIDE: MANAGING ORGANIZATIONAL PROBLEMS OF THE FUTURE

Illustrative of approaches to managing organizational problems may be newly developed techniques to assist the strategic planning process of MNCs. One such approach, developed at the University of Pittsburgh, deserves mention.

MAPS (Multivariate Analysis, Participation, and Structure) enables multinational companies to design alternative global strategies and to evaluate their likelihood of future success. Conceived by Professors Ralph H. Kilmann and Kyung-Il Ghymn, MAPS is based on:

- the participation of company members in defining the specific strategic tasks that they believe would best accomplish organizational objectives;

- the use of multivariate statistics to separate these tasks into clusters of interdependent problems;

- the assignment, using the same techniques, of organizational members into subunits with common preferences on the tasks to be addressed;

- the belief that the allocation of assignments into task clusters and members into subunits is conducive to organization development programs designed to improve organizational effectiveness.[13]

As shown in Figs. 9.1 and 9.2, a twelve-step process is used. However, the most valuable by-product of MAPS analysis is the matching of critical tasks confronting the multinational company

1. Entering and diagnosing the organization.

2. Conceptualizing the design problem and determining the boundaries of the analysis (e.g., who is to be included, which departments, divisions, etc.).

3. Specifying the design objectives (e.g., designing for operational purposes, for strategic planning, etc.).

4. Choosing one of the scientific models of MAPS (i.e., different combinations of input variables, computer analyses, and output formats in relation to design objectives or conceptual models of the problem).

5. Developing the task and/or people items for the MAPS questionnaire (i.e., tasks to accomplish, people to work with on the tasks).

6. Responding to the MAPS questionnaire (e.g., the extent to which each respondent would like to work on each task, and to work with each other respondent).

7. Analyzing the design data from step 6 via the MAPS Computer Program (i.e., using multivariate statistics to generate alternative organization designs by showing which groups of people should work on which clusters of tasks).

8. Selecting a MAPS design (i.e., choosing one of the several designs that can be generated in step 7 via a dialectic debate).

9. Implementing the selected design (i.e., providing resources, authority, policies, responsibility, etc. for members to actually work in new design— team building and support to help them learn to work effectively in new design).

10. Monitoring the implementation process (e.g., assessing resistances to change, emerging problems, etc., and then utilizing strategies to best manage the process).

11. Evaluating the results of the design change (Does the new design solve or manage the initial problem? Does the new design improve organizational effectiveness?).

12. Rediagnosing the organization (i.e., reinstating the diagnostic process in step 1).

Fig. 9.1 The steps of the MAPS design technology. (From Ralph H. Kilmann and Kyung-Il Ghymn, "The MAPS Design Technology: Designing Strategic Intelligence Systems for MNCs," *Columbia Journal of World Business,* Summer 1976, p. 39. Reprinted by permission.)

with interested internal stakeholders. Such a process of commitment building is likely to increase the probability of success in dealing with the complex international business problems that lie ahead.

The MAPS approach is effective in encouraging more systematic and wider participation in solving the chronic problems of multinational corporations. But it is clear that many issues— governmental relations, joint-venture strategies, risk management, and others—require a multiorganizational approach, involving important *external* stakeholders, if any real progress is to be made.

I. *Financial subunit*

(assigned to 13 persons)

Capital availability
Acquisition and merger possibilities
Projection of cash flows
Return on investment
Monetary exchange
Insurance against risks

II. *Political subunit*

(assigned to 10 persons)

Host government political system
Political instability
Relations with neighboring
  countries
Political party factions
Military elite power in politics

III. *Resource/legal subunit*

(assigned to 9 persons)

Restrictions on ownership
Level of industrialization
Raw materials availability
Availability of cheap labor and
  trained management

IV. *Marketing/cultural subunit*

(assigned to 5 persons)

Legal system of host country
Host government attitudes toward
  foreign investment
GNP/per capita income
Market potential

Distribution channel systems
Production costs
Social/cultural factors impacting
  upon products

V. *Legal/economic/political subunit*

(assigned to 7 persons)

Host government attitude toward
  foreign investment
Tax laws
Import/export restrictions
Inflation
Relations with supra-national
  organizations
Technology and its transferability

VI. *Economic/marketing subunit*

(assigned to 3 persons)

Demand and supply conditions
  for the product
Competition
Infrastructure to support business

VII. *Cultural subunit*

(assigned to 7 persons)

Social unrest
Religion/language/racial barriers
Labor organizations
Public literacy
Public attitudes toward foreign
  investment
Living conditions for American
  managers and their families

Fig. 9.2 Matching critical tasks with project participants. (From Ralph H. Kilmann and Kyung-Il Ghymn, "The MAPS Design Technology: Designing Strategic Intelligence Systems for MNCs," *Columbia Journal of World Business,* Summer 1976, p. 44. Reprinted by permission.)

These *multiorganizational problem domains,* as Eric Trist described them, can only be effectively addressed if "all the key stakeholders are in the room."[14] Thus, one of the skills of the social architect of the future will be to help identify the internal and external stakeholders who *ought* to be "in the room" when multiorganizational problem domains are being considered.

Organizational Learning and Social Architecture

Management development in combination with OD offers change agents an important opportunity to effect the social-architectural approach. Recently, for example, we conducted a management seminar designed exclusively to promote understanding between two key internal stakeholders in MNCs: headquarters and subsidiary units. In our opinion, the time had come for a fresh and innovative look at some of the key organizational processes that link headquarters and affiliated companies, and to find new solutions for old problems.

Conducted at the Institute for International Business of the Stockholm School of Economics, the seminar was attended by five major European MNCs, with international business accounting for at least 70 percent of their total sales revenues. Participating companies were encouraged to enroll at least four senior executives— equally divided between headquarters and affiliated companies.

The seminar was designed as a diagnostic and action-oriented experience. Sessions typically contained research findings, cases, and incidents provided by the faculty and participants on various areas of major concern.

The faculty was available throughout the seminar:

- to provide inputs on previous and related research in the key areas of concern;

- to develop scenarios for future political, economic, and social changes affecting the present policies of participating firms;

- to discuss privately unique aspects of each company situation;

- to encourage full and frank discussion among the seminar participants of their own experiences.

The methodology of the course followed a five-stage sequence:

1. *Preseminar meetings and diagnosis.*   Several months before the seminar, faculty representatives interviewed each participating company and, wherever possible, their nominees to the program. To the fullest extent possible, firms were encouraged to enroll only those

executives who would be perceived as legitimate change agents by the company at large.

During this phase, we attempted to gain a broad understanding of each firm's business and organizational dynamics, as well as an appreciation of its problems in managing the linkages between headquarters and subsidiaries. These results were then examined by participating faculty members.

2. *The problem matrix.*   Shortly after the opening of the seminar, the interview findings of the faculty were shared with the participants. In addition, a tentative problem matrix was presented which summarized areas of common and critical importance to all companies. More specifically, three central problem areas emerged:

- The strategic and operational role of headquarters and subsidiaries: How could a subsidiary influence product policy decisions? Should subsidiaries have the freedom to negotiate directly with other subsidiaries without consulting headquarters? To what degree should headquarters intervene in the operational activities of subsidiaries?

- Reporting and control systems: What should be the form and frequency of feedback that subsidiaries receive from headquarters? How could the number of reports between headquarters and affiliates be minimized? How can transfer pricing be used to offer subsidiaries adequate incentives for their efforts?

- Manpower planning and development: How can subsidiary managers reenter headquarters more effectively? How systematic should the career planning process be in MNCs? What is the role of foreign nationals in worldwide companies?

With some fine tuning, the problem matrix was revised to reflect more accurately the concerns of seminar members.

3. *Consulting sessions.*   Subsequently, participants were broken into small consulting teams to work on these three central problem areas for a particular company. In each team, there were representatives from both headquarters and subsidiaries—but from different organizations.

4. *The action matrix.*   After considerable effort, teams presented their tentative action plans to the plenary session. During the critique that followed, their final products were modified substantially.

At this point, teams were reconstructed along strict company lines; and each of the five groups pressed ahead to develop solutions specific to their respective organizations.

5. *The company action plan.*   Finally, the corporate headquarters-subsidiary team of each company presented their action plans to the entire group. After much discussion, appropriate changes were made, and the final document was taken back to the senior management in the company for their consideration.

One participating company, for example, used the finalized action plan as the major agenda theme for its worldwide management meetings, held two months after our seminar. This, of course, sponsored broader organizational commitment for the actions recommended by the seminar respondents; in effect, it legitimatized their role as internal change agents. One year later we participated in a follow-up meeting on the firm's progress in reconciling differences between its headquarters and affiliated companies. Moreover, plans are now underway to conduct similar sessions in affiliated companies.

Single or multicompany seminars of this nature provide an excellent setting to resolve the complex problems confronting the worldwide institutions of today and tomorrow. In addition to the Swedish program, other management development sessions that focus on sharing stakeholders' sentiments in a more systematic manner include:

• The "negotiating game" developed by Ashook Kapoor of New York University. The core of the program consists of specific exercises designed to reduce the difficulties of joint-venture partners from home and host countries.

• The East-West Center's entrepreneurship laboratory. Potential entrepreneurs, multinational executives, regional bankers, and government officials are brought together in Honolulu to build programs that will encourage small-business development in Southeast Asia. Run through the Center's Technology Development Institute, the laboratory has been effective in minimizing the financial problems that, say, a prospective rural hotelier might have in securing a management services contract with a major international hotel system.

• The World Bank's Training Institute offers seminars that enable investors in less-developed countries to encounter their counterparts in the developed countries and international funding agencies. National stereotypes and similar misperceptions are usually dispelled in these meetings. Quite often, viable consortia of national, regional, and international organizations are established in the course of the seminar.

By bringing credible representatives of the key internal and external stakeholders into the room, management development can complement the social-architectural approach to multinational organization development. In the years ahead, we anticipate a rise in such organizational learning.

CONCLUSIONS

One of the authors, Howard Perlmutter, recalls with nostalgia and lasting inspiration a conversation be held with the great social psychologist, Kurt Lewin, shortly before Lewin's untimely death in 1946.

As a young research assistant to Lewin, Howard was interested in the long-term evolution of action research and the problem domains that would need future attention. In a prophetic dialogue, they laid out a scenario that moved action research from its then-timely concern with group dynamics and community development to organization development and multiorganizational development. Lewin's humane perspicacity and his deep sense of what it meant to be a foreigner in a strange land—dimensions not always understood by his compatriots—led him to envisage the kinds of action research that would need attention in the future.[15] The building of international organizations designed to facilitate cooperation and mutual problem solving and discourage national stereotypes seemed imperative.

To be sure, the reality of global interdependence was unclear in 1946, and the brittle character of Spaceship Earth was unknown to most of its inhabitants. To avoid future horrors of the World War

II variety, however, there was agreement that action research would have to adopt a global perspective. In retrospect, it has taken three decades to gain sufficient international experience and to develop the theories, concepts, tools, and techniques needed to facilitate the multinationalization of our corporations, cities, universities, and nation-states.

Accomplishments aside, the majority of social-architectural contributions will be made in the years to come. Needed are new institutions—indeed, new networks of institutions—whose viability and legitimacy are based on a recognition of basic human needs and values. In this regard, the much-maligned multinational corporation, for all its deficiencies, remains one important example of an organization where individuals from many diverse cultures can work together on the basis of their competence, not their nationalities. As an important organizational experiment, the MNC cannot be ignored by other social institutions intent on multinationalization.

For us, the multinationalization process is a *humanization* process, where persons in institutions or networks of institutions collaborate to improve the human condition. This is the fundamental premise of the social-architectural approach to multinational organization development—and, for this reason, it serves as a lasting tribute to the profound humanity of Kurt Lewin.

NOTES

1. "Bennis: Practice versus Theory," *International Management,* October 1975, p. 42.

2. F. E. Emery and E. L. Trist, *Towards a Social Ecology* (London: Plenum, 1972).

3. Daniel Bell, "The New World Disorder," *Foreign Policy,* Spring 1977.

4. Donald A. Schon, *Beyond the Stable State* (New York: Random House, 1971).

5. See Rudlolf W. Knoepfel, "Goals for Global Society," *Planning Review* 3, no. 3 (May 1975): 12; also Karl W. Deutsch, Bruno Fritsch, Andrei S. Markovits, and Helio Jaguaribe, eds., *Problems of World Modeling: Political and Social Implications* (Cambridge: Ballinger, 1977).

6. See Donella H. Meadows, Dennis L. Meadows, Jorgen Randers, William H. Behrens, III, *The Limits to Growth* (New York: Universe Books, 1972); also Michajlo Mesarovic and Eduard Pestel, *Mankind at the Turning Point* (New York: Dutton, 1974).

7. Jan Tinbergen, Anthony J. Dolman, and Jan Van Ettinger, *Reshaping the International Order: A Report to the Club of Rome* (New York: Dutton, 1976). Also, Jan Tinbergen, "A New International Order," *World Future Society Bulletin,* May-June 1976, pp. 7–8.

8. See *The Planetary Bargain: Proposals for a New International Economic Order to Meet Human Needs* (New York: Aspen Institute for Humanistic Studies, 1976.)

9. Jon McLin, "International Institutions for 'Planetary Bargain,' " *American University Field Staff Reports* 10, no. 1 (March 1975): 1–10.

10. Russell Ackoff, "The Corporate Rain Dance," *The Wharton Magazine* 1, no. 2 (Winter 1977): 40.

11. Harlan Cleveland, "How Do You Get Everyone in the Act and Still Get Some Action?" *Educational Record* 55, no. 5 (Summer 1974).

12. Howard V. Perlmutter and E. L. Trist, *Institutions in Crisis: A Social Architectural and Organizational Ecological Approach,* in preparation.

13. Ralph H. Kilmann and Kyung-Il Ghymn, "The MAPS Design Technology: Designing Strategic Intelligence Systems for MNCs," *Columbia Journal of World Business,* Summer 1976, pp. 35–47. See also R. H. Kilmann and B. McKelvey, "The MAPS Route to Better Organization Design," *California Management Review* 17, no. 3 (1975): 23–31.

14. E. L. Trist, "The Concept of Organizational Ecology," Mimeograph, Wharton School, University of Pennsylvania, 1977.

15. A. J. Marrow, *The Practical Theorist: The Life and Work of Kurt Lewin* (New York: Basic Books, 1969).

APPENDIX:
Questionnaires

Questionnaire   *Manpower Managemen*

For each of the Key Decision Areas below you are asked to put the numbers in the boxes and circles according to the followin; classification:

☐   Present approach (1 = best description; 2,3 = also describing present policies and practices, if any, in *decreasing* order o relevance).

○   Suggested approach (1 = first best alternative; 2,3 = second, third best alternatives, if any).

Avoid any irrelevant choices.

KEY DECISION AREAS

MANPOWER PLANNING

Forecasting Personnel Needs	☐○ Corporate, international, and/or regional headquarters forecast the majority of the management needs of our subsidiaries.	☐○ Our subsidiaries forecast the majority of their respective management needs. Very little liaison exists with corporate, international, and/or regional headquarters or other overseas companies in making these forecasts.	☐○ Our subsidiaries' management needs are forecast by collaborating with regional headquarters and local subsidiaries.	☐○ Our subsidiaries management need are forecast by col laborating with cor porate, internation al, and/or regiona headquarters as wel as other subsidiaries
Job Descriptions	☐○ Job descriptions in our subsidiaries generally emphasize home-country requirements—for example, U.S. management ability for the American multinational company.	☐○ Job descriptions in our subsidiaries generally emphasize needs relevant to the local country—for example, local management ability.	☐○ Job descriptions in our subsidiaries generally emphasize needs relevant to our regional area—for example, Spanish management ability for our LAFTA companies.	☐○ Job descriptions ii our subsidiaries gen erally emphasiz neither home-coun try nor national cri teria but rathe cross-cultural an international abili ties.

MANPOWER ADMINISTRATION

Recruitment Criteria	☐○ In our subsidiaries, we seek skills, background, and personality traits in an individual most compatable with the parent company standards.	☐○ In our subsidiaries, we seek skills, background, and personality traits in an individual most compatible with the local environment—for example, graduation from a Grande Ecole, elite family background, etc.	☐○ In our subsidiaries, we seek skills, background, and personality traits in an individual most compatible with the regional environment—for example, Spanish heritage.	☐○ In our subsidiarie: we seek out thos managers with hig potential as inter national managers a well as managers i the host countrie:
Identification of Prospective Managers	☐○ In our subsidiaries, we use home-country methods in identifying prospective managers—for example, executive search, references from home-country subsidiaries in a local country, etc.	☐○ In our subsidiaries, we use local identification methods for the most part—for example, contracts in government departments.	☐○ In our subsidiaries, we use regional identification methods for the most part.	☐○ In our subsidiarie: we use a number c identification tech niques based on ou experiences aroun the world.

Screening Methods	☐○ In our subsidiaries, we rely heavily on parent company screening methods. Application forms, interview procedures, etc., were designed by the parent company.	☐○ In our subsidiaries, we rely heavily on local screening methods, uniquely designed for each particular country.	☐○ In our subsidiaries, we rely heavily on regional screening methods for our local company.	☐○ In our subsidiaries, we use a mix of parent company and local techniques—for example, our application form is based on experience in many countries.
Selection	☐○ Prospective managers in our subsidiaries are most often selected on the basis of their compatibility with the parent country—for example, previous work experience in the parent country is considered very important.	☐○ Prospective managers in our subsidiaries are most often selected on the basis of their compatibility with the local marketplace.	☐○ Prospective managers in our subsidiaries are most often selected on the basis of their compatibility with the regional market.	☐○ Prospective managers in our subsidiaries are most often selected on international potential—the ability to perform well in a number of overseas markets as well as in a local subsidiary.
Assignment **1. Foreign Service**	☐○ Prime positions in our subsidiaries are staffed with citizens of the parent country or, to a lesser extent, third country nationals.	☐○ Prime positions in our subsidiaries are staffed by local nationals.	☐○ Prime positions in our subsidiaries are staffed by regional citizens.	☐○ Nationality makes no difference in our key subsidiary positions. Competence, not passport, counts.
2. Regional Headquarters	☐○ Prime positions in our regional headquarters are staffed with citizens of the parent nationals because they are considered more effective.	☐○ Prime positions in our regional headquarters are staffed from a country within our region.	☐○ Prime positions in our regional headquarters are staffed with citizens from our region.	☐○ Key regional headquarters positions are held by nationals of all countries.
3. International Headquarters	☐○ Prime positions in our international headquarters are staffed with parent nationals because they are considered more effective.	☐○ Prime positions in our international headquarters are staffed with parent nationals because foreign nationals do operate better in their home countries.	☐○ Prime positions in our international headquarters are staffed with parent nationals because foreign nationals, especially those from certain regions, operate better in their own regional countries.	☐○ Key international headquarters positions are held by nationals of all countries.
4. Corporate Headquarters	☐○ Prime positions in our corporate headquarters are staffed with parent nationals because they are considered more effective.	☐○ Prime positions in our corporate headquarters are staffed with parent nationals because foreign nationals do operate better in their home countries.	☐○ Prime positions in our corporate headquarters are staffed with parent nationals, especially those from certain regions, operate better in their own regional countries.	☐○ Key corporate headquarters positions are held by nationals of all countries.

Development

Assessment Criteria	☐ ○ In our subsidiary, we emphasize personality traits most compatible with the home country criteria of success.	☐ ○ In our subsidiary, we emphasize local norms as the most useful measure of a man's success.	☐ ○ In our subsidiary, we emphasize a man's ability to work in a regional environment as being most important.	☐ ○ In our subsidiaries, we emphasize a man's ability to work in a multinational environment as being most important. For example, how well can he motivate people of all nationalities?
Performance Appraisal	☐ ○ In our subsidiaries, we rely heavily on parent-based methods for assistance in performance appraisals.	☐ ○ In our subsidiaries, we evaluate management personnel with locally-designed techniques.	☐ ○ In our subsidiaries, we evaluate management personnel with regionally-designed techniques.	☐ ○ In our subsidiaries, we are using a variety of evaluation methods with no particular national identification.
Training Objectives	☐ ○ We are providing training opportunities for nationals from our country to make good assistants for parent company executives in our company.	☐ ○ We are providing training opportunities for nationals from our country to reach key positions in our country, but not in other companies.	☐ ○ We are providing training opportunities for nationals from our country to reach key positions in our company, other regional companies, and regional headquarters.	☐ ○ We are providing training opportunities for nationals from our country to reach key positions anywhere in the world.
Training Programs	☐ ○ We generally use training programs in our subsidiaries that have been successful in the parent country.	☐ ○ Our training programs have been locally-designed for local conditions.	☐ ○ Our training programs have been locally-designed for regional conditions.	☐ ○ Our training efforts incorporate a number of various national approaches using a design which is universally valid.
Promotion	☐ ○ In our subsidiaries, parent country citizenship or, at least, experience or know-how is highly valued in one's promotion.	☐ ○ In our subsidiaries, we identify advancement with knowledge of local conditions. Generally, vacant top-level positions are filled by nationals.	☐ ○ In our subsidiaries, we identify advancement with knowledge of regional conditions. Generally, vacant top-level positions are filled by nationals from our regional area.	☐ ○ Promotability in our subsidiaries depends on one's ability using worldwide standards of competence and not one's national origin.
Termination	☐ ○ In our subsidiaries, we terminate most management people because of their deficiencies in parent company managerial standards.	☐ ○ In our subsidiaries, we terminate most management people because of their deficiencies in local managerial standards.	☐ ○ In our subsidiaries, we terminate most management people because of their deficiencies in regional management standards.	☐ ○ In our subsidiaries, we terminate most management people because of their inability to be effective managers using worldwide standards.

Compensation

Salary Policy	☐ ○ In our subsidiaries, we offer parent country expatriates (and some 3rd country nationals) a number of complex differentials—overseas premium, housing allowance, etc. Nationals are generally paid in accordance with local conditions.	☐ ○ In our subsidiaries, we pay going local salaries for all management personnel irrespective of passport; no differentials awarded.	☐ ○ In our subsidiaries, we pay going regional salaries for all management personnel irrespective of passport; no differentials awarded.	☐ ○ In our subsidiaries, we pay a global (not local) standard to all our managers for similar positional responsibilities. No discrimination exists between foreign and indigenous management.

Incentives Policy	☐◯ In our subsidiaries, we offer the most attractive fringe benefits to expatriate managers—for example, liberal home leave vacations.	☐◯ In our subsidiaries, we offer only those incentives which enable us to be competitive with local industry, e.g., local pension privileges.	☐◯ In our subsidiaries, we offer only those incentives which enable us to be competitive with regional industry, e.g., regional pension privileges.	☐◯ In our subsidiaries we offer any incentives needed to attract and retain managers from each country in the world. For example, we allow participation in a global pension system.

MANPOWER CONTROL

Inventory	☐◯ Few indigenous personnel of our subsidiaries are recorded in corporate, international, and/or regional headquarters management inventory. Expatriate managers are invariably included.	☐◯ In our subsidiaries, we maintain local personnel inventories. No interchange of management information exists with corporate, international, and/or regional headquarters as well as other foreign subsidiaries.	☐◯ In our subsidiaries, we maintain a regional personnel inventory. No interchange of management information exists with corporate, international, and/or subsidiaries of other regions.	☐◯ In our subsidiaries, we are part of a multinational inventory designed to facilitate worldwide management development.
Audit and Review	☐◯ Corporate, international, and/or regional headquarters maintains extensive controls over our subsidiaries' manpower management. Frequent supervisory visits occur by headquarters personnel teams.	☐◯ The emphasis in our subsidiaries is on local control of each subsidiary's manpower audit and review. Contact with corporate, international, and/or regional headquarters is infrequent.	☐◯ The emphasis in our subsidiaries is on regional manpower audit and review. Contact with corporate, and/or international headquarters is infrequent.	☐◯ An integrated, global program exists between our subsidiaries and all headquarters with respect to manpower audit and review of the personnel function, not only of our subsidiary but also other subsidiaries and corporate, international, and/or regional headquarters (usually through a multi-national task force).

Advantages and Disadvantages of   *Manpower Management*
Present and Suggested Profiles

Please examine the profile of your answers on the manpower questionnaire. Listed below are possible *advantages* and *disadvantages* of the present and suggested approach. Insert numbers 1 through 5 in those captions that you consider most relevant to your company—in *decreasing* order of importance. If any unlisted advantages or disadvantages apply, describe and rank them accordingly under the "other" caption. Focus on the overall manpower pattern—not on any one particular manpower decision area.

A. Present Approach

Most important *advantages* of present approach

☐ Simple organizational design—easy to administer

☐ Increased profitability through reduced costs

☐ Greater sensitivity to local needs

☐ Other. Please specify:

_____

_____

_____

Most important *disadvantages* of present approach

☐ Nonoptimal use of global resources

☐ Distrust created between managers

☐ Problems of communication and coordination

☐ Lack of group-wide comparisons

☐ Other. Please specify:

_____

_____

_____

B. Suggested Approach

Most important *advantages* of suggested approach

○ Better allocation of global resources

○ Broader global outlook and image

○ Improved interchange of information

○ Increased group profitability

○ Other. Please specify:

_____

_____

_____

Most important *disadvantages* of suggested approach

○ Increased bureaucracy

○ More expensive

○ Insensitive to local conditions

○ Limited number of suitable managers

○ Other. Please specify:

_____

_____

_____

Internal Obstacles to   *Manpower Management*
Internationalization Process

Please list the five most critical internal obstacles which, in your opinion, prevent or hinder your company from becoming a truly international firm. What actions do you recommend be taken by your company to reduce these obstacles?

Internal Obstacles	*Recommend Actions*
1. _____	To reduce obstacle 1: _____
_____	_____
_____	_____
2. _____	To reduce obstacle 2: _____
_____	_____
_____	_____
3. _____	To reduce obstacle 3: _____
_____	_____
_____	_____
4. _____	To reduce obstacle 4: _____
_____	_____
_____	_____
5. _____	To reduce obstacle 5: _____
_____	_____
_____	_____

Potential Objective Measures to
Monitor Internationalization Process

Manpower Management

Please list possible objective or quantitative measures on which your company should be assessed annually in order to determine its progress in becoming a truly international company. For example, you might choose "Nationality of persons who hold key positions in International Headquarters" as a *dimension*; 50% of key positions by foreign nations as a *target*; and ten years as a realistic *time perspective*.

Dimension	*Target*	*Time Perspective*
1.		
2.		
3.		
4.		
5.		

SELECTED BIBLIOGRAPHY

Aharoni, Y., "On the Definition of a Multinational Corporation," *Quarterly Review of Economics and Business* 2 (1971), p. 14.

Alderfer, C. P., "Organization Development," *Annual Review of Psychology* 28 (1977), pp. 197-223.

Ansoff, H. I., R. P. Declerk, and R. L. Hayes, *From Strategic Planning to Strategic Management* (New York: Wiley, 1976).

Apter, D. E., and L. W. Goodman, eds., *The Multinational Corporation and Social Change* (New York: Praeger Publications, 1976).

Argyris, C., *Intervention Theory and Method: A Behavioral Science View* (Reading, Mass.: Addison-Wesley, 1970).

_____, *The Applicability of Organizational Sociology* (Cambridge, Mass.: Cambridge University Press, 1972).

Argyris, C., and D. A. Schon, *Theory in Practice: Increasing Professional Effectiveness* (San Francisco, Calif.: Jossey Bass, 1974).

Barnet, R. J., and R. E. Mueller, *Global Reach: The Power of the Multinational Corporations* (New York: Simon and Schuster, 1974).

Bateson, G., *Steps to an Ecology of Mind* (New York: Ballantine, 1972).

Beer, M., and E. F. Huse, "A Systems Approach to Organization Development," *Journal of Applied Behavioral Science* 8, no. 1 (1972), pp. 79-101.

Bell, D., *The Coming of Post-Industrial Society* (London: Heinemann, 1974).

_____, "The New World Disorder," *Foreign Policy,* Spring 1977.

Bennett, P. W., "Participation in Planning," *Journal of General Management,* Autumn 1974.

Bower, J. G., J. L. Franklin, and P. A. Pecorella, "Matching Problems, Precursors, and Inverventions in OD: A Systemic Approach," *Journal of Applied Behavioral Science* 11 (1975), pp. 391–410.

Burke, W. W., and H. A. Hornstein, *The Social Technology of Organization Development* (Washington, D.C.: NTL Learning Resources Corporation, 1971).

Davis, S. M., "Trends in the Organization of Multinational Corporations," *Columbia Journal of World Business* 11 (1976), pp. 59–71.

Dror, Y., *Ventures in Policy Sciences* (New York: Elsevier, 1971).

Dunn, E. S., Jr., *Economic and Social Development—A Process of Social Learning* (Baltimore, Maryland: Johns Hopkins, for Resources for the Future, Inc., 1971).

Dunn, W. N., and F. W. Swierczek, "Planned Organizational Change: Toward Grounded Theory," *Journal of Applied Behavioral Science* 13, no. 2 (1977), pp. 135–157.

Dymsza, W. A., *Multinational Business Strategy* (New York: McGraw-Hill, 1972).

Emery, F. E., and E. L. Trist, *Towards a Social Ecology* (London: Plenum Publications, 1972).

———, "The Causal Texture of Organizational Environments," *Human Relations* 18 (1965), pp. 21–32.

Fouraker, L. C., and J. M. Stopford, "Organizational Structure and the Multinational Strategy," *Administrative Science Quarterly* 13 (1968), pp. 47–64.

Friedlander, F., "OD Reaches Adolescence: An Exploration of Its Underlying Values," *Journal of Applied Behavioral Science* 12 (January–February–March 1976), pp. 7–12.

Friedlander, F., and L. D. Brown, "Organization Development," *Annual Review of Psychology* 25 (1974), pp. 313–341.

Friend, J. K., and W. N. Jessop, *Local Government and Strategic Choice* (London: Tavistock Publications, 1969).

Galbraith, J. K., "The Defense of the Multinational Company," *Harvard Business Review* 56 (1978), pp. 83–93.

Habermas, J., *Knowledge and Human Interests* (London: Heinemann, 1972).

Heenan, D. A., "Global Cities of Tomorrow," *Harvard Business Review* 55 (1977), pp. 79–92.

_____, "The Corporate Expatriate: Assignment to Ambiguity," *Columbia Journal of World Business* 5 (1970), pp. 49–54.

_____, *Multinational Management of Human Resources: A Systems Approach* (Austin, Texas: University of Texas, Bureau of Business Research, 1975).

Heenan, D. A., and C. Reynolds, "RPO's: A Step Toward Global Human Resources Management," *California Management Review* (Fall 1975), pp. 5–9.

Hirschman, A. O., and C. E. Lindblom, "Economic Development Research and Development Policymaking: Some Converging Views." In F. E. Emery (ed.), *Systems Thinking* (Harmondsworth: Penguin, 1969).

Hornstein, H. A., and N. M. Tichy, "Developing Organization Development for Multinational Corporations," *Columbia Journal of World Business,* Summer 1976, p. 136.

Huse, E. F., and M. Beer, "Eclectic Approach to Organizational Development," *Harvard Business Review* 49 (September–October 1971), pp. 103–112.

Hymer, Stephen, "The Multinational Corporation and the Law of Uneven Development." In J. N. Bhagwati (ed.), *Economic and World Order From the 1970's to the 1990's* (New York: MacMillan, 1972), pp. 113–145.

Kahn, R. L., "Organizational Development: Some Problems and Proposals," *Journal of Behavioral Science* 10, no. 4 (1974), pp. 485–502.

Kilmann, R. H., and K. Ghymn, "The MAPS Design Technology: Designing Strategic Intelligence Systems for MNCs." *Columbia Journal of World Business* (Summer 1976), pp. 35–47.

Kingdon, D. R., *Matrix Organization: Managing Information Technologies* (London: Tavistock Publications, 1973).

Maisonrouge, J., "The Mythology of Multinationalism," *Columbia Journal of World Business* 9 (1974), pp. 7–12.

Mintzberg, H., "Strategy-Making in Three Modes," *California Management Review,* Winter 1973, pp. 44–53.

Pate, L. E., W. R. Nielsen, and P. C. Bacon, "Advances in Research on Organization Development: Toward a Beginning." In R. L. Taylor, M. J. O'Connell, R. A. Zawacki, and D. D. Warrick (eds.), *Academy of Management Proceedings '76* (Proceedings of the 36th Annual Meeting of the Academy of Management, Kansas City, Mo., August 11–14, 1976), pp. 389–394.

Perlmutter, H. V., "The Multinational Firm and the Future," *The Annals of the American Academy of Political and Social Science,* September 1972, pp. 139–152.

_____, "The Tortuous Evolution of the Multinational Corporation," *Columbia Journal of World Business* 4 (1969), pp. 9–18.

_____, *"Towards a Theory and Practice of Social Architecture: The Building of Indispensable Institutions* (London: Tavistock Publications, 1965).

Perlmutter, H. V., and D. A. Heenan, "How Multinational Should Your Top Managers Be?" *Harvard Business Review* 52 (1974), pp. 121–132.

Perlmutter, H. V., and E. L. Trist, *Institutions in Crisis: A Social Architectural and Organizational Ecological Approach,* in preparation.

Rhenman, E., *Organization Theory for Long Range Planning* (London: Wiley, 1972).

Rose, S., "Why the Multinational Tide is Ebbing," *Fortune,* August 1977, pp. 111–120.

Rutenberg, D. P., "Organizational Archetypes of a Multinational Company," *Management Science* 16 (1970), pp. 337–349.

Schmuck, R. A., and M. B. Miles, eds., *Organizational Development in Schools* (Palo Alto, Calif.: National Press Books, 1971).

Schon, D. A., *Beyond the Stable State* (New York: Random House, 1971).

Sirota, D., "The Multinational Corporation: Management Myths," *Personnel* 49 (1972), p. 37.

Sirota, D., and J. M. Greenwood, "Understanding Your Overseas Work Force," *Harvard Business Review* 48 (1971), pp. 56–59.

Soleri, Paolo, *Arcology: The City in the Image of Man* (Cambridge: MIT Press, 1971).

Starbuck, W. H., ed., *Organizational Growth and Development* (Harmondsworth: Penguin, 1971).

Thompson, J. D., "Technology, Polity and Societal Development," *Administrative Science Quarterly* (March 1974), pp. 6–21.

Vaill, P. B., "Practice Theories in Organization Development." In J. D. Adams, ed., *New Technologies in Organization Development* (La Jolla, Calif.: University Associates, 1974), pp. 71–84.